Katherine Stannard

THE WILLIAM JAMES LECTURES

Delivered at Harvard University

1961–1962

Gabriel Marcel

THE
EXISTENTIAL BACKGROUND
OF
HUMAN DIGNITY

Harvard University Press

Cambridge, Massachusetts

1 9 6 3

Printed in the United States of America

To Henry Bugbee and Hubert Dreyfus,
whose friendly help has been invaluable,
with my affectionate greetings

Contents

The Existential Background of
Human Dignity

I ◄

Introduction

W HEN I was invited by Harvard University to deliver the William James Lectures for the year 1961,
I felt immediately that it was impossible for me to decline such
a flattering proposal. First of all, it would give me a unique
opportunity to make myself heard in the United States and
to establish contact with the intellectual élite in this country.
It would also offer an opportunity to repay to a certain extent
the debt I contracted long ago toward the American philosophers of the beginning of this century. Here I allude to William James himself, to Josiah Royce, and to William Ernest
Hocking, who honored this University for so long, and whose
book *The Meaning of God in Human Experience*,[1] published
shortly before World War I, influenced me so deeply that I
dedicated my *Metaphysical Journal*, published in 1927, to him,
as well as to Bergson. Hocking and I had corresponded on
several occasions during the last thirty or forty years, but it
was only in 1959 that I had the great good fortune of meeting
him in his delightful Madison home, located in a countryside
which ranks among the most beautiful I have ever seen, and
is one of the most appropriate for enriching the contemplative
thought of a man who, through the visible world, has never
ceased to have the presentiment of what is eternal. This meet-

[1] New Haven: Yale University Press, 1912.

1

ing proved to be a memorable event for me; it was as if a blessing had affixed its seal upon it.

Before endeavoring to describe in broad terms the debt I contracted long ago toward American thought in its newest and most forceful aspects, I should like to say first of all that this thought brought a breath of freshness and life to the arid world of speculation that was mine during the years just preceding World War I, when I was a prisoner of post-Kantian German philosophy in its most abstract forms. True, I was an impatient prisoner, even inclined to revolt, but I still did not possess the philosophical equipment capable of transforming into reality what was then only a predisposition, or a vague uneasiness of mind.

It goes without saying, too, that at that time I had already been strongly marked by Bergson, whose courses at the Collège de France I attended with passionate interest. However, I do not believe that I am mistaken when I say that I should not have been able to learn from him the beginnings of existential philosophy which I discovered through contact with the philosophers of this continent.

I referred earlier to a breath of freshness, and indeed it is on this idea of freshness that I must insist at the very beginning of these lectures. For the conflict between freshness and staleness has, to a great extent, ordered the whole development of my philosophical thinking. What I appreciate so much in William James is precisely that he appears to have felt in the highest degree the need that has become increasingly insistent in my own case—to struggle relentlessly against the peril to which all thought is exposed: that of becoming rancid, like butter, or overripe, like fruit. This need has never ceased to stimulate my own thinking.

Undoubtedly, later on, and in connection with concrete examples, especially concerning values, I shall have the opportunity to return to this point and to examine the nature of this process. But it seemed pertinent at the very beginning to point out what, for me, is a major concern.

Furthermore, a thing I have so often experienced in life has once more been verified; namely, that a call, which at first we might be tempted to say was sent from without, has had the eminent value of inciting me to accomplish certain work which, left to myself, I might not have had the strength or the heart to undertake. But in the perspective that I have chosen it is perhaps a mistake to introduce here the idea of exteriority. I am deeply convinced that the contacts that play such a decisive role in the life of any creator can be really understood only if they are interpreted in terms of a certain logic, immanent as well as transcendent, without which all creation worthy of the name is quite inconceivable. This means that we must be careful not to speak of chance in such a domain. It is certainly not by chance that in 1949 and 1950 I should have been invited to deliver the Gifford Lectures at Aberdeen, this call having enabled me to achieve the approximate synthesis constituted by the two volumes of *Le Mystère de l'être*. I believe that it is not by chance either that Harvard University should have sent me a similar call some ten years later; or that I should have become conscious of the task confronting me today in order to answer this call, and face this task in proportion to my strength—now, unfortunately, declining. In short, this means that the destiny of a philosopher, or an artist, or a scientist, implies a type of interplay, very mysterious and unforeseeable as to its effects, between what one might call his psychological individuality and an environment from which he can be isolated only by abstraction.

Immediately after deciding to accept the University's invitation, I clearly saw that these lectures should be concerned with the problem of man considered in the anguished context of today's world. At first, I succumbed to the fear of becoming involved in a too ambitious undertaking which would exceed

my capacities. Thus my first intention was to limit myself to
the development, although greatly expanded, of the lecture I
delivered at Saint-Gallen, in Switzerland, in June 1960, on the
"Problem of Man in Contemporary Philosophy since Bergson
and Nietzsche." This, I thought, would have the advantage
of enabling me to find shelter, so to speak, among the philosophers whose thought I would have to expound, with the
possibility of entering in personally in the concluding lectures
in order to indicate as clearly as possible how my own position
differed from or approached that of Scheler, Buber, Jaspers,
or Heidegger.

On reflection, however, it appeared to me that this would
not only show a lack of courage, but that it would in a certain
way frustrate the expectations of my audience. When I was
honored with this invitation, it was surely not to hear me ana-
lyze or even comment in detail upon the system of thought
of such and such a philosopher concerning whom many others
have or could have spoken with a competence probably
superior to mine. Thus, I decided to commit myself more
personally and deeply in what I shall call this adventure. The
word "adventure" may seem surprising at first; however, it
corresponds to reality. For reasons those acquainted with my
work may probably suspect, and for other motives which will
appear much more clearly later on, it was and had to be out
of the question for me to present anything that might resemble
a sort of didactic treatise presented in installments. I could
not have done so without betraying a certain fundamental
intention which has asserted itself more and more explicitly
in my writings, ever since I understood that I could not and
would not bring forth a system that would perhaps be doomed
to dry up rapidly like so many others. Even before the 1914
War, but much more distinctly during and after it, the notion
of research compelled my attention, a type of research that,
however much one pursued it, however much it became conscious of its own meaning, remained nevertheless, and had to

remain, research. Yet there was no question of converting it into a body of propositions capable of being set up for all time and recognized as true, except as regards the mental processes by which these propositions were arrived at. Thus, it is not at all by chance that my thought should have been expressed for a long time in diary form. However, I should hasten to add that this was only one of its modes of expression. Although traditional philosophers would certainly be unwilling to admit this, it is undeniable that my dramatic work, far from constituting an entirely separate compartment of my life, completes indissolubly my philosophical or, I might say, technical writings, whether in diary or lecture form. In reality, my dramatic work constitutes a vital element of the research which I might say has been my unique vocation since that distant period when I started to become conscious of my self. I shall, in fact, have occasion to return to this point many times, because my plays, which are very little known in the United States, might be compared to an underground stream whose overflow, often scarcely perceptible, irrigates, as it were, my speculative thought.

But here I should like to specify as clearly as I can what the term *philosophical research* represents for me. It is sufficient to concentrate one's attention, as should always be done, I believe, on the terminological equivalents of the word "research" in different languages, to realize that we must place ourselves within a certain zone of indetermination. The German word *Versuch* emphasizes the element of attempt or trial that is implied here; whereas the English term *inquiry* aims rather at what would be in the nature of an investigation or questionnaire. It might be well, therefore, for us to examine rapidly—or rather to review—the different registers in which the verb *to search* may be used.

The most elementary and undoubtedly the least instructive case is the one related to something lost which must be found. It seems to me that the English expression *to look for* corre-

sponds to this case. I look here and there in the hope that the
lost object will come to my attention. After locating it, I
exclaim: "Here it is!" As a rule, this search will proceed at
first according to a certain method. Reflection shows me that
the object searched for can have been lost only since such and
such a day, or that moment, or at this or that place, upon
which my investigation will focus. Only if it fails do I despair
and begin searching almost haphazardly. In so elementary a
case as this there is no doubt about the nature of the object
being looked for; there is doubt only about the conditions
under which it disappeared, since I might, for instance, ask
myself if it had been stolen, by whom, for what reason, and
so forth.

Thus it is easy to go from this example to the more complex
case of criminal investigation. Here again it is a question of
finding out something and not inventing it, although, as we
shall see, even this distinction tends to disappear. The problem
consists of locating the thief or the murderer, because we are
certain such a person exists. But in this case it is obvious that
the search cannot be carried out haphazardly, and we see
those responsible for it engaged in a type of mental activity
that is, properly speaking, not unrelated to the creative effort.
Inevitably, the time comes when Sherlock Holmes or Hercule
Poirot must work out a hypothesis to orient his action, at
least temporarily. Moreover, this hypothesis can assume form
only after a complete inventory of the data has been made.
The hypothesis will then be used as a point of departure to
ask a certain specific question of what we very vaguely call
reality. We must, therefore, proceed in such a way that reality
will be forced to answer without any possible ambiguity.
Thus, everything will occur as though a real dialogue were
taking place between the investigator and reality. Moreover,
we should have to try to make out what is hidden beneath a
word as vague and general as "reality." It is applied to a certain
body of persons and things bound to one another by relation-

ships that will assume form only progressively. It will have been indispensable to circumscribe this body—the way a piece of territory is circumscribed—in order to limit the number of investigations to be undertaken. It will also have been necessary to ensure the justifiable exclusion of the possible appearance of an unknown element not figuring in the body under consideration. So long as this appearance cannot be rationally ruled out, the investigation will be carried on within an indeterminate area.

But we must realize that whatever the complexity of the situation faced by the investigation, it remains within a certain field of vision. Here, as in the case of something that has been lost, we are obliged to proceed in such a manner that what we are looking for finally emerges before our eyes under conditions that permit us to exclaim at last: "Here it is!"

But if we consider now what constitutes research on the technical level, it will differ from the cases just described, except perhaps in the area of prospecting, where it is intended, for example, to reveal the existence in this or that region of, let us say, a certain metal or a particular source of energy. But I believe the words *technical research* are not applicable here in their full meaning. In my opinion they generally express much more the invention of a certain process designed to meet a specific need in an area which is, properly speaking, that of industry, provided the word industry be taken in a sufficiently broad meaning.

There is, however, something in common between technical research and that previously described. There is of course no longer any question of discovering or locating an object or a cause, but there is one of meeting a need. In both cases, however, the search seems to be controlled by an idea that exists in the mind of the searcher.

It is possible, however, that this idea may lose its clear outlines, as in the case of explorations carried out in a completely unknown country. Here we might almost say that it is a

matter of finding even before searching, or, to be more accurate, of knowing what we are looking for. We should not
fail to note either the sense of joyous freedom that accompanies exploration, insofar as it excludes nearly all preconceived ideas and consequently the always rather painful tension attached to expectation of something specific, and the
anxious confrontation of what is anticipated with what is
actually found. When the search is centered on a definite
object, as in prospecting, everything that is not this object is
dismissed as irrelevant. For the explorer, on the other hand,
everything that comes into view is in some way welcome and
appears as a sort of gratuitous gift which is like an enrichment
for him who finds and receives it. Here I refer to something
each one of us may have experienced well this side of exploration as we understand it. This is the experience of the ecstatic
walker—the adjective in this case assuming definite value in
conformity with etymology—who feels drawn outside himself by everything that meets his eye.

In this connection I believe that it is very important to insist
upon the original nature of the attitude we assume when we
set out on a voyage of discovery, with no idea of devoting
ourselves to any utilitarian pursuit—that is to say, to the
pursuit of an aim or of a specific object.

But here a comment seems necessary. This receptivity, this
avid readiness to accept anything that turns up, is usually to
be found in children who, when confronted with objects as
well as words, are not yet blasé. That is to say, the edge of
their thirst for knowledge has not yet been taken off, as it
almost certainly will be, alas, later, when they will have been
through school. For then they will be burdened with a knowledge they were not taught beforehand to seek for themselves
or even to desire. Furthermore—and we must not overlook
this point—therein lies the reason why this will constitute
only pseudo-knowledge, the contrary of true knowledge,
which is the fruit of internal, organic growth.

The explorer's position, therefore, in whatever domain, seems to me to resemble to a certain extent that of the child who has not yet been to school. In any case, discovery will be sought for its own sake and will reward the often painful effort that, in addition, enhances its value. We come now to one of the most disinterested, freest activities that exist, and, I might add, one that can make the greatest contribution to the flowering of the human spirit. Moreover, it may be said, that this activity is nearly always destined to give rise to still another type of activity which consists in exploiting for specific aims the results to which it has aspired.

From my own experience, I shall not hesitate to declare that the impatient ardor that actuates the philosopher-apprentice is not in itself absolutely different from that which we admire in the explorer, or simply in the child, in whom there quivers a sort of impatient, universal curiosity. The philosopher-apprentice, at least in the beginning, also feels that he is destined to discover virgin lands; indeed, he realizes that he must make his way in a world which seems at first to be entirely different from the field of his manoeuvres thus far. As a result he will often experience, to begin with, a sense of intoxication that will be all the purer since his teacher—if he is wise—will refrain from overwhelming him with a technical vocabulary comparable to that in which he was initiated, for instance, in mathematics. He will start, therefore, with the exhilarating sensation of being at once at home and in an unknown country, where everything remains to be discovered without any visible obstacle standing in the way of his progress. However, we should add that, except in one of those privileged cases when the original grace we call vocation has been granted him, he will usually be quickly disappointed. He will notice that in answer to the questions his teacher has led him to put to himself in his own way—when the teacher is capable of this—not only does everything seem to have been said already, but "solutions" that appear to be

completely contradictory have been offered by philosophers
of apparently comparable reputation. Consequently, not only
will it seem presumptuous on his part to attempt to form a
personal opinion on these much-debated questions, but he will
also have the impression that these opposite solutions neutralize
one another, that a sort of hopeless greyness overlies the whole
length and breadth, as it were, of the philosophical landscape.
However, it would be more accurate to acknowledge that this
word "landscape" is no longer suitable, and that the student
has instead the impression of being in a sort of work-yard
strewn with objects the use of which he no more understands
than does a stranger walking among the factories and ware-
houses in an industrial center grasp the meaning of what he
sees. His initial interest has therefore died down; for him everything has become merely examination material and he will be
content to do the subaltern philosophical work that consists
of learning by heart stereotyped answers to questions that will
be asked him on the fatal day by some sullen-faced professor.

But the true philosophical vocation manifests itself first of
all through the rather mysterious power of resisting this type
of disillusionment. Furthermore, it is necessary to point out
that the professor of philosophy, when he is equal to the task,
will do his best to sustain and, as it were, nourish this resistance
in the few students he has discovered who give any sign of
possessing this uncommon gift. It may be added that the philosophical vocation does not necessarily imply either the intention of devoting oneself to teaching philosophy, or a desire
for specialization of any kind. On the contrary, it may very
well happen that for some reason the man who has chosen
this career gives absolutely no sign of possessing such a vocation. This applies to innumerable students who, every year,
prepare a licentiate's certificate in a university, and have ac-
quired in the process a certain smattering of psychology or
metaphysics. In fact, I should be inclined to deny that the
word "smattering," when applied to specialized knowledge,

could be used in this case to designate anything of significance. But this leads me to specify more precisely than I have done thus far just what constitutes this vocation.

Here I believe we should refer to a fundamental experience which in some way was presupposed in what went before, and that is the experience of wonderment, or, more precisely, of the *thaumazein* of the Greeks, which lies on the borderline between wonderment and admiration. I do not mean by this the wonderment caused by a specific phenomenon—as, for instance, an astronomic phenomenon such as an eclipse, or the appearance of a shooting star—whose nature the scientist will be able to explain, or at least define, more or less accurately. In this case, wonderment will disappear once a satisfactory explanation has been given. But it stands to reason that this explanation will always be of a particular nature. We might say that it will be given within a certain concrete totality, which in itself will remain outside its grasp, or at least will stem from a general and inevitably contested hypothesis which, contrary to the specific explanation, will necessarily allow the original wonderment to subsist. Since I cited the example of astronomic phenomena, I am very naturally reminded of passages from Pascal's unforgettable *Pensées:* "I see the frightening spaces of the universe confining me, and I find myself bound to a corner of this vast expanse, without knowing why I am in this place rather than in another, or why this short time granted me to live has been assigned to me at this point rather than at another of the eternity that preceded me and all that will come after me. In every direction I see only infinities that confine me like an atom and like a shadow that lasts only a moment, never to return." Supposing that a general hypothesis should succeed in accounting for the motion of heavenly bodies, it is quite obvious that it would be incapable of putting an end to the fundamental wonderment expressed in a text such as the one I have just quoted, or in the following one: "When I consider the short duration of

my life absorbed in both the preceding eternity and the one
to come, the small space I occupy and even see engulfed in
infinite immensity, spaces of which I am ignorant and which
know nothing of me, I am frightened; and I wonder at finding
myself here rather than there; why now, rather than then.
Who put me here? On whose order and under whose guidance
were this place and this time assigned to me?"

I shall be expressing a conviction that has remained unshakable with me for more than half a century when I say
that a philosopher remains a philosopher only so long as he
retains this capacity for wonderment in the presence of certain fundamental situations, despite everything surrounding
and even within him that tends to dispel it. I am thinking first
of all of the sort of agnostic resignation that he will have occasion to inhale like a vapor and which, like a kind of atmos-
pheric blight, can even affect the vividness of his original
aspiration. What is the use in exerting oneself, along with
many others, in an attempt to elucidate what no one has ever
succeeded in making intelligible? Do not the sterile efforts of
so many eminent men prove that this search is a vain one;
that either it is meaningless, or else our structure excludes the
possibility of reaching a valid conclusion in this domain: that
is, a conclusion capable of compelling universal recognition?
However, any philosopher worthy of the name refuses to
bow before this demurrer opposed to his inner exigency. For,
in reality, this exigency comprises specifications that correspond to the philosopher's own personality. I shall show as
clearly as possible how, in my own case, little by little, this
need asserted itself and assumed precise outlines.

Generally speaking, no doubt, we may say that it is a question of a demand for intelligibility; only we should immediately observe that the Greeks long ago, and perhaps even more,
the Moderns, felt the need to clarify increasingly the nature
of the act of comprehension itself and to discover not only
what it consists of, but also how what we call reality lends

itself to such operations, and within what limits. We might say more broadly that the principal characteristic of the philosophical mind consists in constantly restricting the scope of what is taken for granted. Thus the wonderment I mentioned earlier becomes a sort of challenge.

Nevertheless, I believe I must add the following: at times this questioning activity may end by being used with a sort of blind obstinacy; and if it takes this direction, it can degenerate into a mechanical process and, as a result, tend to lose its own dignity.

Here the problem I consider to be essential claims our attention: that of the relationship between philosophical research and life. We shall see later the central position it has occupied in my work, and, further, that it remains in the foreground of my immediate concerns.

It is a fact—and here I refer again to my own experience—that a young man who feels the call of the philosophical vocation I spoke of earlier, may very well launch forth into metaphysical speculation even before living it. I can still hear my venerable teacher, the sociologist Lucien Lévy-Bruhl, telling me one day, perhaps to encourage me—I must have been nineteen or twenty years old at the time: "There are two domains in which it is possible to be creative very early: mathematics and metaphysics." And it is indeed true that mathematics has witnessed many precocious geniuses such as Pascal, Evariste Galois, or Abel, all of whom made decisive discoveries. To a certain extent, too, the same holds true in respect to several German metaphysicians: here I am thinking of Schelling's or Hegel's early writings. I must admit, however, that at my present advanced age, I am inclined to consider somewhat warily any philosophical thought which its author has been so bold as to formulate before having had genuinely lived experience. I say "genuinely" because there is always the experience of others as conveyed through books. This borrowed experience, however, is never anything but a substitute, imperfect and to a certain extent dubious, for true experience.

Furthermore, I fear that it might be necessary to give up entirely the concept so clearly formulated by Descartes of a *tabula rasa,* arrived at by a deliberate effort of rational thinking and from which, for instance, it would be possible to proceed in order to reconstruct synthetically what the philosopher Hamelin has called in our time "the main elements of representation." Even supposing that such an attempt were possible, we should doubtless be obliged to say that it was accomplished in the past as well as could be and that there is probably no reason to try to renew it. Nor does it seem to me that the philosopher has the slightest interest in copying the mathematician's method as Spinoza did, for instance—I mean classical mathematics, of course, because present-day mathematics has achieved an extremely strict analysis of what in the past appeared to the geometrician as pure evidence or pure rudiment. In fact, in the next chapter I shall attempt to show according to which inner logic in my case the experience was, so to speak, reaffirmed within a system of thought which seemed to scorn it. In geological terms, what really matters is to point out the successive sedimentations, or layers, as a result of which my mental soil has become what it is today, since to some extent this soil must give sustenance to the remarks I shall make later. These remarks will center on the problem of man, a problem which I have already said is fundamental and impossible to elude. As we shall see, however, the preceding statement calls for a correction, because it will appear clearly that we are witnessing today an almost systematic effort to do away with this problem. But this operation cannot be carried out without endangering what we have thus far considered to be essential values. Indeed—and this will not be the easiest part of my task—I shall perhaps have also to show that this past phase of my research, far from constituting an inert deposit, or a devaluated, obsolete currency, should be considered rather as having become a horizon, a beyond in which past and future meet to enter into a dimension which is no longer that of life perceived merely as sequence or as the fall of leaves.

At the close of this first chapter, I believe it might be useful to quote a text which was to appear in my first *Metaphysical Journal*, and which I took up later in *Homo Viator*. It seems to me that this text expresses in a manner that is both accurate and synthetic the direction of the movement that ever since my first philosophical stutterings, has borne me—and I insist on this point—not toward the elaboration of a system, but toward articulation of a certain utterance I can only call increasingly my own if I add immediately that a sensitive ear will perceive in it a sort of secret quaver: the quaver of a man who dreads above everything else giving in to a presumption to which the philosopher can succumb only too easily; of a man who is aware that he is making his way along a narrow path between deep chasms, toward an end which is not of this world, but without which this world would become engulfed in pure nonsense.

Metaphysical disquiet.—It seems to me that a metaphysical system is nothing if it is not the act by which a disquiet is defined and succeeds partially—as well as mysteriously—if not in abolishing, at least in transposing or transmuting, itself into an expression of self that, so far from paralyzing the superior life of the spirit, on the contrary, strengthens and maintains it.[2]

Here I shall interrupt my quotation to ask myself the exact meaning of the expression "superior life of the spirit." For I must admit that today it seems too vague to me and at present I would not use it spontaneously. I believe that it refers to self-control, in a broader sense of the term than the commonly accepted one. This is the self-control that gives the philosophies of the past their importance. This does not imply, however, that we should necessarily subscribe to them as systems.

[2] *Metaphysical Journal*, trans. Bernard Wall (London: Barrie and Rockliffe, 1952). Quotations from this work are from the English edition.

There is nothing, or nearly nothing, in the writings of Plato or Descartes, Kant or Hegel, that does not deserve the most serious attention, precisely because these great minds have established themselves on a plane which infinitely transcends the level of arbitrary, changing opinions, set forth by men who never express themselves otherwise than superficially. I believe too that the great works of imagination to be found on the outskirts of philosophy, not only those of the best in literature but those of the great composers as well, offer this same characteristic, this sort of specific gravity; and we can only pity those persons who today are unable to appreciate it. Later, we shall have occasion to point out some of the pernicious influences that operate against this faculty.

After this parenthesis, which seems indispensable to me, we return to the text I started to quote earlier.

What are we to understand by this disquiet? First of all, it is not a form of curiosity. To be curious is to proceed from a certain motionless center, to tighten in order to seize an object concerning which one has only a confused and schematic mental image. In this sense, all curiosity is outward bound. On the contrary, however, to be anxious is to be unsure of one's center; it is to be in search of one's own balance. The following is true in any case; if I am anxious about the health of someone close to me, my resulting apprehension really tends to destroy my inner stability. The more the object of its concern is a close part of myself, the more intimately it is incorporated in my inner structure, the more my curiosity will tend to become anxiety. On the other hand, the anxiety I feel is all the more metaphysical inasmuch as its object cannot be separated from me without I myself being annihilated. It is doubtless true to state that except for the problem of "what am I?" there are no other metaphysical problems, since in one way or another, they all lead back to it. And in the last analysis, even the problem of the existence of other conscious beings is reduced to it. Indeed, a secret voice I am unable to silence assures me that if others are not, then neither am I. I cannot grant myself an existence, while accepting that others be deprived of it; and here "I cannot" does not mean "I have not the right," but rather, "it is impossible for me." If others elude me, then I elude myself.

Can I say that I feel this metaphysical disquiet in the form of an immediate reaction, such as that we experience, for instance, when waiting for a loved one who is slow to arrive? I do not think so. I should be more inclined to say that circumstances may, and even must, inevitably arise in which I shall become aware of an anxiety which appears, upon reflection, to extend infinitely beyond these circumstances themselves, for it possesses a permanent nature, in that it is not bound to this or that *present.* Furthermore, as soon as it is formulated, it extends to all the beings whom I may consider to be participating in the same experience that I am. It is anxiety for all of us; and this is tantamount to saying that it is not at all a question of man in general—a mere fiction invented by a certain rationalism—but rather of my brothers and myself.[3]

Need I say that this last sentence furnishes to a certain extent the keynote, in the musical sense of the word, of all the research to come, and that it enables us to see in what perspective the problem of man today will be approached. We might, if need be, and with certain reservations, speak of an existential anthropology as opposed to an anthropology that would be a discourse on the essence of man or on human nature. But at the same time the fragment that comes to a close with that sentence will make it possible for the reader to understand why, in the chapters to follow, it seems absolutely necessary for me to retrace as accurately as possible the various stages of the sinuous road I have had to follow for the last forty years. I shall also refer constantly, as I go along, to the dramatic works that have marked my way.

[3] *Homo Viator,* trans. E. Craufurd (London: Gollancz, 1951). Quotations from this work are from the English edition.

II ≺

Participation

To avoid any confusion, it may be worth mentioning at the outset what perspective I intend to take in retracing the main stages of my thought over nearly half a century. I have a very definite aim in retracing the way I have taken. I want to try and throw some light on the undeniably tragic situation in which modern man finds himself today when he attempts to reflect on what I think I must call his vocation. I speak of his vocation and not of his nature, for the particular disciplines concerned with "man's nature" threaten to dissolve it into an infinite number of different components, each one of which, far from being a separate element endowed with an intrinsic reality of its own, is in turn dependent upon a whole complex of factors apart from which it cannot be conceived. Hence in talking of man's nature we risk an infinite regress which is bound to appear to a person as an outright dissipation of what he would spontaneously mean in speaking of his substance or of his own being.

I must first point out a strange contrast between the present-day world and the world which presented itself to me in about 1910. As a young Frenchman belonging to cultured middle-class circles, I was, on the whole, more concerned with safeguarding the existing order and fundamental liberties than with establishing a stricter social justice, which often seemed to me to be inseparable from a suspect demagoguery and from a leveling of society to the advantage of the mediocre. In spite of serious shocks, which may have been recognized here and there as ominous, the world in those days could very well be regarded by an inexperienced observer as established for a long time to come. Those illusions now appear to me in retrospect as little short of absurd. Except for what certain young people were doing in taking a militant part in revolutionary trade union activities and in the Action Française, French political life at that time was indeed a stultifying affair; I could find nothing in it to excite my interest. I vividly remember my astonishment on learning that a friend of mine, whom I very much respected, approved of the civil servants' first strike which took place at about that time. I cannot think of a better way than this to show the narrow confines in which my imagination was working. I was repelled by the spectacle which parliamentary life afforded as well as by the periodic administrative crises. I saw the banal and featureless part of Paris in which I lived as an outward expression of a dehumanized, colorless world in which greatness and the tragic had no place. In revulsion from such pedestrian surroundings my thought soared toward metaphysics.

I must also point out that apart from Bergson's lectures at the Collège de France, which I followed with a passionate interest and admiration, the official philosophy of the time was not a great deal more inspiring than the political life. But as compensation we did have the history of philosophy taught us by such brilliant men as Victor Delbos, and for me this was like a window opening upon other horizons. For reasons which I am not sure that I can make out with complete clarity even now and which might in part derive from my German ancestry—my grandparents on my mother's side were Jewish and came from near Mainz—it was German philosophy of the most abstruse kind which first aroused my interest. It is true that I was rather quickly to turn toward Anglo-Saxon thought, but only toward that school which, from Coleridge to the neo-Hegelians of the day, had been influenced by thinkers on the other side of the Rhine. It now seems to me, when I recall this stage of my philosophical development, that what attracted me about these philosophers was what seemed to me to be the rigorousness of their thought and, at the same time—and certainly more than any other factor—their ability to surpass and transcend everyday life and all its monotonous round of trivial and exacting concerns.

At this point in my retrospect I find myself up against an anomaly which was to be such a decisive factor in all that was to follow that I feel I must pause to dwell on it. This will to surpass or to transcend which the post-Kantian thinkers encouraged in me ran almost contrary to another disposition of mine; and perhaps in this connection my paternal heredity played a relevant part. My father, a man of the very widest culture, whose like I have since rarely met and who held extremely important positions—in particular in the administration of the Beaux-Arts—had the most lucid, the most exact mind. There is no doubt but that in the world, such as he saw it, art was of supreme importance, though he had at the same time a passion for history. He was horrified by anything vague and woolly and his intellectual integrity was exemplary. He loved to read aloud and did it remarkably well, and it was he who initiated me into many plays, and perhaps contributed decisively to my love of the theater. And so, in opposition to the strong metaphysical tendency in me, there developed an increasingly explicit refusal to abstract from all the concrete detail of my life that detail which made my life my own in all its irreducible originality.

Thus a tension developed between these two poles which is evident in even the earliest of my essays. Abstraction, far from appearing to me as an end in itself, presented at best a steep and tortuous path which it was of course necessary to follow, but only in order to come eventually upon the genuinely concrete—a concrete more effectively such than sensory experience, wherein sensory experience would doubtless reappear, but transformed and transfigured.

I need hardly mention that the movement of thought that I have just characterized is the same as Bradley's. I shall never be able to say to what precise extent the author of *Appearance and Reality* [1] contributed to the formation of my thought. But without questioning Bradley's influence in any way I may say that the drift of his thought answered to a fundamental concern already manifest for a number of years—not in my philosophic thinking, but in the working out of my plays. From childhood I was attracted to dramatic art, along with music. I loved music passionately and even dreamed of devoting my life to it. That was before I had seriously approached philosophy. It is clear that in my own case this love of the theater and music implied both a passionate interest in individual beings and an irresistible attraction toward reality in its inexhaustible mystery. I think I can say without hesitation that it is music, and music almost exclusively, which has been for me an unshakable testimony of a deeper reality in which it seemed to me that everything fragmentary and unfulfilled on the sensory level would find fulfillment.

Now it was precisely my problem to reconcile these aspirations, which could not help but appear contradictory at first. I began with abstract rigorous thought of which I found noteworthy examples in the post-Kantians, though they could not satisfy me completely. It became necessary to break a path by which I could reflectively rejoin what had been given me more or less immediately in dramatic experience or in musical intuition. I have said that I was concerned with breaking a path. Perhaps it would be better to speak of digging a well. A few months ago as I was rereading—often with

[1] Francis H. Bradley, *Appearance and Reality: A Metaphysical Essay* (London: S. Sonnenschein, 1893).

a measure of exasperation—my youthful philosophical writings about to be published at Louvain,[2] I felt as if I were present at a drilling operation performed by unskilled hands and primitive instruments. As is often the case, these writings only become clear in the light of the thinking I was to carry out much later. I do not wish to reproduce here the dialectics which I then developed and which today I by no means judge as irreproachable. But in order to show the later development of my thought, I shall have to sketch very briefly some of the positions with which I was then occupied.

In an essay which I wrote in 1911, a few months after my passing my *agregation de philosophie*, I came to grips with the Hegelian idea of Absolute Knowledge, and even the idea of Absolute Experience, in which Bradley's philosophy, at least at the time of *Appearance and Reality*, reached its culmination. What I set out to show was that neither Absolute Knowledge nor Absolute Experience could be regarded as a self-sufficient whole and so could not be the source of a legitimate abstraction. This was the very thinking in which the demand for such a self-sufficient whole was being pressed, without conceiving any place for itself in that whole. The mistake seemed to me to consist in hypostatizing what is after all only a requirement of thought and in believing it possible to isolate and consider the product of this act as a reality in itself. The philosophers of Absolute Knowledge seemed to be victims of the same illusion as the Naïve Realists: "They believe," I wrote, "that they can sever the bond which unites the object (in this case Absolute Knowledge) to the subject and treat the object as a separate being, without perceiving that the reality in question owes its being to the participation of the one who is thinking it. Absolute Knowledge, like Matter or like Life, is still only an abstraction, although indeed the highest and most concrete." [3]

[2] *Fragments Philosophiques, 1909–1914.*
[3] *Ibid.*, p. 43.

It will be noted that I have used the term *participation*—an expression which occurs more and more frequently in my early writings. With this theme I set out upon the path which Louis Lavelle was later to take; but I hasten to add that this distinguished man, in taking this path, was to evince an ability to systematize which I myself have never possessed.

Before going into what I mean by participation I must bring up another matter which comes out quite clearly in these initial investigations—namely, that we have an unavoidable tendency when speaking of the human subject to objectify him, and so to convert him into a pure abstraction, thereby missing the inexhaustible wealth of what Maurice Blondel was later to call "la pensée pensante." Subsequently, I attempted to show that it is indeed through the subject that we must try to understand how we participate in being, but only on the condition that the subject be reinstated in his reality as subject, apart from all misleading objectification. At the same time I continued to insist on the freedom which then appeared to me as coextensive with the subject himself and as susceptible of affirmation only beyond the confines of any possible positive knowledge. On the other hand, in accordance with that concern which brought me into touch with religious thought, I attempted to find in participation in being a principle, which, if not identical with faith, was at least open to it—at a time when I had not the slightest notion of joining the Church or any desire to do so. It is important to point out that I was living then in agnostic circles and had received no religious education. My father, who came from a Catholic family, had detached himself from all matters of religious belief early in his life. My aunt, who had brought me up after the death of my mother, which occurred when I was nearly four, and who had then married my father, was also an agnostic, but in a very different sense. I can say without exaggeration that if my father belonged to the aesthetic stage (in Kierkegaard's view), my aunt in turn had a purely ethical point of view, and a profoundly pessimistic one at that, as far as mankind and life were concerned. For my aunt—who gave me an unsurpassable example of moral integrity—in a world subject, it seemed, to the caprices of blind forces of which the prospect was enough to awaken in the soul a despair which knew no refuge, there was but a single guiding light, one fixed star: this was moral certainty, conceived as both an unfailing respect for truth and as action directed unremittingly toward the service of others and toward the succor of the disinherited. I do not think I am mistaken in saying that the contrast, which at times was almost overpowering, between these two visions of the world —a contrast which I deeply felt rather than noted—was the source of the mysterious but irresistible current which carried me toward that third stage, which is neither purely aesthetic nor purely ethical, but religious. But at the same time I was too deeply influenced by the circles in which I lived and by the negative convictions of my relatives not to regard with the greatest mistrust the cults celebrated in the churches or in the chapels which I entered only occasionally. I remember very well on seeing Venice for the first time—I was then about ten—how proud I was to have visited with my father some twenty churches where I admired the Carpaccios, the Titians, the Giovanni Bellinis, and so on; but I saw the churches themselves only as museums and I was not in the least interested in the anachronistic and, to me, incomprehensible rites which were practiced in them. What is most surprising, and what I now find hard to understand in retrospect, is that religion, considered in itself and in what might be termed its transcendence, appeared to me as being essentially untainted by those blemishes which mark the history of cults. To account for this paradox I can only form hypotheses.

Beyond all question the sudden death of my mother gave me a lasting shock and aroused in me an anxious questioning. I could not tolerate the equivocal position into which my family seemed to fall. I clearly recall a certain walk with my aunt when I must have been about seven or eight, during which my aunt, having told me that no one could know if the dead were completely annihilated or lived on in some way, I exclaimed: "When I'm older I'm going to try to find out!" And I think it would be a mistake to take those childish words lightly: in some way they determined the course I was to take.

But this is not an adequate explanation of the sort of existential assurance by which I came to recognize a mysterious primacy in religion. The vague term "primacy" is used advisedly here; the word "value" would be out of place, and at the time of which I am speaking—the year 1911–1912—I would have rejected it categorically. But to complicate the matter still more, neither would I have accepted the word "truth" used in this connection. At that time in fact, I was convinced that an idealist like Leon Brunschvig was right in insisting upon a strict connection between truth and verification. It seemed to me reasonable to suppose that we would be entitled to speak of truth only where verification was possible and our powers of demonstration could be brought into play. Thus, I was irresistibly led to affirm the existence of a region beyond the verifiable which would be the province of religious thought. I speak of "religious thought" because it is clear that as far as I was concerned religion, if it were not to degenerate into practices fit only for sociological study, would have to remain thought. And the modalities of such thought were what I set out to explore. The difficulty with which I had to cope was that of conceiving an order which, while irreducible to any objective constituents, would in no way be tainted by an arbitrariness commonly believed to prevail on the level of subjectivity. Thus, with the rudimentary instruments at my disposal, it was a question of setting off in the direction taken by Kierkegaard, whom I then knew only by name, for the two or three pages devoted to him by Hoffding, the philosophical historian whose text I had consulted, had in no way allowed me to suspect what might have been the main intent of this man of genius.

When I refer to that early period of my thought, my attempt to conceive participation as transcending positive knowledge appears as an anticipation of the insight which came to me a little later that existence precisely cannot be reduced to objectivity.

But I think I should also say that the assurance of which I have spoken was actually given me above all by music. In music I found a mysterious and unshakable testimony: A musical phrase by Bach or Beethoven—and here I mean almost exclusively the Beethoven of the last period—seemed invested with a supreme authority which did not allow of any explanation. One was beyond knowledge and yet it was as if one breathed a certainty which went infinitely beyond the limits of a simple, individual emotion deriving from a particular temperament or sensitivity. The greatest musical works seemed to invoke directly a certain communion. I speak of communion, for each of those involved is not just anyone, and still less are these individual representatives of thought in general, of the *Denken uberhaupt* of Kant and the Kantians. Perhaps it is the reference to this type of universality in the individual which must be kept in mind if we wish even to glimpse the meaning of the inquiry in which we are engaged.

Some of the early texts which I have been reviewing—especially the sketch for "Théorie de la Participation"—must be read in the light of these preliminary explanations. "Participation," I wrote,

is not a fact, not a mental endowment, it is a requirement of free thought, a requirement which becomes actual in posing itself, since its realization does not depend on any extraneous condition. We can, however, distinguish two stages of participation, according to whether it is defined as an object of thought, or whether thought, renouncing its function as a thinking subject, gives itself wholly to participation:

this second phase alone deserves to be called Faith: Faith is in a certain sense more than an immanent act since it is the accomplishment of a dialectic wholly directed towards transcendence. It is manifest, moreover—and it is thus that its transcendence is to be defined—that this Faith can in no way make itself explicit in a judgment, even in a judgment of existence, for the subject which makes judgments of existence is already engaged in existing . . . Faith is thus not the affirmation of an existence; the problem of the existence of God—a problem completely devoid of metaphysical meaning—could only have occurred to a crude intellectualism imprisoned in empirical modes of thought concerned with contingent objects. Maimonides was right in pointing out that existence could not possibly apply to God.[4]

We may recall that this position was reassumed at the end of the nineteenth century by Jules Lagneau, who was the teacher of the philosopher Alain,[5] and also of Leon Brunschvig. It should be clear that the text I have quoted is not to be construed in any way as atheism. On the contrary, my concern was to find a possible way of safeguarding the reality of God, which appeared to me to be inevitably compromised from the moment one speaks of His existence; I thought one might speak of the existence of only that which falls within the purview of experience. In this there was a Kantian echo, to be sure. But what was constantly at stake, even in this infinitely rarefied atmosphere, was to safeguard what from then on appeared to me of supreme importance—I mean love, and love understood in the deepest, widest, and least psychological sense. Today I consider all this research—in itself so confused and so clumsily carried out—interesting only because of the intention behind it and because of the underlying experience which I have attempted to evoke.

On the other hand, what seems to me now to be still worthy of interest is the way in which, on the dramatic level, I tried to counteract this almost bloodless speculation; and in this con-

[4] *Fragments*, p. 93.
[5] Pseudonym of the French philosopher Emile Auguste Chartier (1868–1951).

text I feel I must deal with the two plays which I published
in the same period, during the winter of 1913–1914, under the
title of *Le Seuil invisible*.

It goes without saying that within the limits I have set myself
it is not from the playwright's point of view that I shall consider these two plays, or those that I shall treat later. I will say
only that these plays had much in common from the technical
point of view with the post-Ibsen theater, and especially with
the work of François de Curel, an author who is today wholly
neglected but who, at the beginning of the century, enjoyed
the greatest respect, especially among intellectuals.

In *La Grace*,[6] written in 1910–1911, I showed the conflicts
between an intellectual young woman with an uncompromis-
ingly rational mind, Françoise, and Gerard, her husband, who
became converted to Christianity under what seemed to her
to be highly questionable conditions; in fact, Gerard, having
discovered before his marriage that he was suffering from a
lung infection, had wanted to break the engagement. But the
young woman, passionately, physically, in love with him, had
refused. She married him and left with him for the mountains, doing everything that might restore his impaired health,
only to realize with horror that a kind of spiritual gulf was
forming between them. She has no doubt whatsoever: it is
Gerard's illness which accounts for his religious evolution. He
is looking for everything that life denies him on the earthly
level in an imaginary God. I will not go into the action in
detail, but I would like to point out that in this play I was
attempting to bring out the ambiguity of a situation which
allows of two different and irreconcilable readings: that of the
psycho-physiological materialist, and that of the mystic for
whom this illness, far from being a cause, is a providential
occasion which the subject's creative freedom renders viable
for faith. To Gerard, Françoise, whom he had first sincerely
loved, becomes the temptress whom he must resist. At a cer-

[6] Published in *Le Seuil invisible*.

tain point he comes very close to yielding to this temptation, but Françoise, who is a deeply sincere human being, confesses that in her distress and because of her despair over the gulf widening between her and Gerard she has given herself to another man whom she did not really love. Gerard feels her betrayal as somehow providential, and following her admission he regains possession of himself, and her attraction for him fades. As he lies dying, Françoise's young brother, Olivier, who is not a believer but who is repelled by materialism, comes to testify to his affection for Gerard. He tries to join Gerard in the faith to which he, Olivier, aspires, but which he is not yet able to share. I will quote here the last few lines of the play, the implication of which will be clear:

Olivier. Somehow your faith seems to be more than a truth; it is an act, a creation; it is like an idea which transforms and realizes itself . . . No? Still more? I still feel that what I say leaves you uneasy.
Gerard (indistinctly). And God?
Olivier. Is He spirit affirming its unity? Is He self-transcending faith . . . Even more? I can't follow you . . . Perhaps He is only man's supreme longing.
Gerard (raising himself with effort). God is free! [7]

Then he dies, and Olivier, searching in anguish for the mystery of his peaceful countenance, murmurs: "And now this look alone remains, and only on the faith in this look . . ."

It will be seen readily enough that Olivier sums up in a few words the very thought I was then trying to develop along the lines of participation. But Gerard—in crying "God is free!"—puts himself beyond this world of mere thinking. Thus the dialogue between Olivier and Gerard transposes to the human level, in a context that can already be called existential, the sort of hesitation which my philosophical writings then showed. I was hesitating between an idealism to which I still remained faithful and the trend of my thought toward transcending this idealism in the direction of an attempt to

[7] *La Grace* in *Le Seuil invisible*, p. 208.

reinstate existence, an attempt which was to take place under circumstances which I will discuss later on.

Reference to the final pages of "Théorie de la Participation," to which I alluded earlier in this chapter, and which dates from the winter of 1913–1914, will reveal that the affirmation of divine freedom is clearly to be found there—but in what context?

I had already tried hard to show that it would not be legitimate for thought, operating in the name of universal principles, to consign the concrete and individual actually sustaining it to a merely contingent status; that our thinking, on the contrary, must acknowledge the noncontingency of this experience if it is not to become inconsequential. But this brings us back, I continued, to regarding this experience as subject to a higher power and this is essentially what the believer understands by divine will. To transcribe this into the personal language that I use when I meditate on my own experience: I find myself in strictly determined circumstances regarding my birth, the milieu in which I live, the people I have met, and so on . . . It would be altogether inadequate to maintain that these conditions are due to pure chance and for that reason, insignificant. It is in relation to them that I have to exert my freedom, and in the course of doing so I am led to appreciate my circumstances as having been—in the strongest sense of the word—given. In this way I came to think of a will which is giving and at the same time free.

I must admit that this whole discussion, into the details of which I cannot enter, now seems very shaky to me: In the first place, it seems to me doubtful whether the line of thought I have just been sketching can hold good beyond the level of an "as if"; I must consider my experience *as if* the conditions in which it develops had been given me by divine will. Moreover, this very affirmation of divine will depends on the subject who makes it. Now, it is clear that the believer—like Gerard in *La Grace*—holds, on the contrary, that divine freedom is strictly independent of the act which affirms it. And it is just this inward division on my part which the closing scene of the play shows. On the philosophical level I was certainly aware of it, but at the same time I tried to overcome it through a dialectic which remained subject to idealist principles.

But I was, to some extent, to go beyond this idealism in my play *Le Palais de sable,* written two years after *La Grace* but never performed, although in my opinion it is of a much higher quality than the play of which I have just spoken. The action takes place shortly before the first World War in a French provincial town. Roger Moirans, the central character of the play, is a politician, a conservative who is dedicated to defending the rights of Catholicism against free thought. He has set himself up as the champion of traditional morality and has just achieved a great success in the city council where he has attacked the secularism of the public schools. It is natural enough under such circumstances that he should be opposed to the divorce of his daughter Therese, who wants to leave her unfaithful husband and start her life afresh. In this instance he proves himself virtually heartless; all his tenderness goes out to his second daughter, Clarisse, whom he takes to be spiritually very much like himself. But now Clarisse tells him that she has decided to take the veil and become a Carmelite. Moirans is horrified by the idea that this creature, so lovely, so intelligent, and so full of life, might go and bury herself in a convent and he decides to do his utmost to make her give up her intention. But Clarisse is stunned to see how passionately her father fights against what she believes to be her vocation; the way in which he talks about convent life seems to her to be incompatible with a Catholicism worthy of the name. Her astonishment is all the greater since, after all, it was her father who taught her the awareness of God. He is, then, going to be forced to recognize and to admit that the taste he has always had for religion, for religious traditions and attitudes, is not an authentic faith, since the sacrifice which Clarisse is longing to make appears vain and devoid of any true meaning for him. The fact is that he does not believe in the other world where her sacrifice would find its full justification. It is not too much to say that belief in the world to come, in eternal life, seems to him to be a myth and basically absurd. For Moirans, religion has always been equivalent to a faith which in some way sustains itself through its own ardor, but is dependent on no transcendent reality. In a word, he is obliged to recognize that he is only a religious dilettante. And at this decisive moment, in which the fate of the only being in the world whom he really loves is in question, he is compelled to recognize how hollow and divorced from life his religion is.

Clarisse is deeply shocked; her father now appears to her as an impostor, virtually as a deliberate fraud, and she finds herself faced with an agonizing dilemma: she begs her father to stop setting himself up as the champion of a religion in which he does not really believe and to withdraw from political life; it seems to her that this is the price he must pay to save his soul. But Moirans answers her cynically, saying that he will consent only if she gives up her intention of entering the convent. And suddenly a pall of confusion settles upon the unfortunate Clarisse: she begins to wonder if what she has believed to be her vocation is not a temptation and if she is not bound to repudiate the call which she believed to be addressed to her by God. She tries in vain to find the solution by consulting a priest who is wholly incapable of understanding her problem. And everything happens now as if she had been in some way contaminated by her father's thought. The stupid things which the priest says in answer to her questions suddenly make convent life appear in a sinister light. She convinces herself that her duty lies in yielding to her father's wishes and at the same time in making him put an end to a ghastly comedy.

And so, apparently, Moirans is triumphant, but at what

price? He would now like Clarisse to marry a young doctor who has for a long time been in love with her and for whom she does have a genuine respect. But Clarisse cannot bring herself to marry him. She has put the convent behind her but she retains, if not nostalgia, at least the sense of an incompatibility between her own being and the so-called normal life of a woman who is to marry and have children. She is, it seems, condemned to live from now on with her father, straying somewhere between heaven and earth. And her father, in these circumstances, is led to make an observation which shakes him to the core: he had always, in the manner of the idealists, held that each one of us is perfectly alone in life and that isolation is, as it were, the price paid for freedom. But this really only obtains for someone incapable of love. From the moment that one human being loves another a solidarity is created between the two. Moirans has not been able to prevent his daughter's depending on him, and because of this he has given her a real power over him. "And so," Moirans exclaims, "is autonomy itself to be an illusion and is one not even to have the right to think one's own thoughts? Can it be that I have invested another with this terrible power of depending on me?" And Clarisse answers, "At last, Father, you do understand me. Yes, *you* gave me this terrible power." Moirans reproaches himself for not having respected Clarisse's faith; but she responds, "Perhaps that moment of feverish concern on your part came nearest to something like love in your life. For at that moment you felt the weight of loneliness and you suffered."

Moirans. Yes, but why did you have to be the victim of this suffering?
Clarisse. The fruitless sacrifice of a life was perhaps necessary to expiate for your having walled yourself in; for you have lived a solitary life among men.
Moirans. In what possible realm does this mysterious notion of yours hold good?
Clarisse. It is a realm that we can affirm simply on the strength of our being able to think of it.

Moirans. And yet if it is not willed by any God?

Clarisse. Father, remember: our thoughts must be capable of sufficing
unto themselves; they emanate from no center. They reflect no
world apart from them.

Moirans. Ah yes . . . I recognize now what I once thought so wise.
Why does it seem so different now?

Clarisse. Because it is something you've lived through.[8]

It is obvious that Clarisse has succumbed to the temptation
of an idealism that is nothing but a degeneration from an authentic faith which is in itself prereflective. Certainly we are
not here in the presence of a thesis disguised as a play. No conclusion is, nor can be, imposed on the audience. What *is* presented here as a definite reality is the bond between beings—
what I later came to call "intersubjectivity"; in this sense the
play anticipates what is to follow.

Perhaps I should add one further remark about the play:
Moirans appears as utterly blind; his blindness is that of the
idealist whose thought obstructs communication with other
people by preventing him from even imagining them in their
concrete reality. Thus we come upon one of the basic ideas
of my work, and one to which we shall return in different
contexts: self-consciousness, far from being an illuminating
principle, as traditional philosophy has held, on the contrary
shuts the human being in on himself and thus results in opacity
rather than enlightenment.

[8] *Le Palais de sable,* pp. 389–390.

III ◂

Existence

THE writings to which I have so far referred date from before the first World War, and so does the first part of the *Metaphysical Journal*, where a sort of drilling operation is tentatively carried out toward a goal which I should not have been able to define with any precision at the time. It was, in fact, a question of an exploration in the sense I have already defined, with all the uncertainties and hazards that such an exploration implies. From my present perspective I am struck by the fact that this research was directed less toward man or the human than toward an effort to see how a certain metaphysical reality could be, if not grasped, at least approached. In an article published in 1912 entitled "The Dialectical Conditions of the Philosophy of Intuition," [1] I attempted to show that intuition, contrary to what Bergson had contended, could not be self-warranting, and that only reflection might perhaps, under certain conditions, confirm its value.

But what strikes me most forcefully today is that all these investigations developed out of what I should perhaps now call a certain existential security. I am not alluding here to the fact that I belonged to well-to-do circles and that the question of my daily bread did not bother me unduly. I refer rather to the fact that in spite of the several shocks I have mentioned,

[1] *Le Revue de Métaphysique et de Morale*, Paris, 1912.

my world—*our* world for us artists, writers, and philosophers
—still did not seem to be either seriously or vitally threatened.

From this point of view the date, August 2, 1914, truly
marks the transition from one world to another.

I do not propose to retrace my thoughts and emotions during the war. It seems only necessary to say this: on the one
hand I do not think that I ever doubted the justice of the position which was ours as Frenchmen or that of the Allies in the
conflict, even if I was later brought to recognize that at least
on the Russian side everything was not so pure as I had at first
naïvely supposed. But on the other hand, from first to last,
I felt intimately concerned in this immense tragedy and judged
severely, as did all my relatives, the attitude of Romain Rol-
land and his pretense of keeping himself above the fray. And
so, for the first time, I faced the issue of commitment, which
was much later to become a focus for my reflection. I must
add that for reasons of health I had not been called up; unable
to bear the idea of being an outsider, I had joined the Red
Cross, to which I devoted a part of my time throughout the
war. Far from clashing with my genuinely philosophical activity, this Red Cross work involved a task of reflection the
results of which were to have considerable importance. The
principal object of my work was to give information to those
families who came to ask for news of soldiers reported missing,
that is, of those who did not appear among the dead, the
wounded, or on the lists of prisoners-of-war. Whenever I
could, I made a point of seeing personally those who came to
make inquiries and, far from treating them as mere cases from
the files, did my best to show them the greatest possible sympathy. This gave me the opportunity of coming into contact
with many people from all walks of life and of making a constant effort to put myself in their place, in order to imagine
the anguish which they all shared but which underwent subtle
transformations in each of them. It is against this background

of deep distress that each questionnaire, each inquiry, stood out.

Interrogating, making inquires, and responding—these were my activities, and, as a philosopher, I tried to throw some light on them.

When I refer to my *Metaphysical Journal*, however, I note with astonishment that it is not until July 23, 1918, that this reflection on the questioning activity is formulated: "What is interrogation? It is an effort to correct a state of relative indetermination." "Every question," I said, "implies a disjunctive judgment, the affirmation that only one of the alternatives is true or valid; the recognition of inability to determine *which* alternative, if the subject is thrown back on to his own resources." I am confined to my bed, I cannot see what is happening outside and I ask: "Is it raining?" The disjunctive judgment is: it is either raining or it is not, but I am not in a position that allows me to decide for myself. So I ask someone who is in a different position and who is able to inform me.

It would be advantageous, perhaps, to point out that in many cases disjunctive judgment, far from being reduced to such a simple form, has an indeterminate and practically infinite multiplicity—for example, if I ask someone: "What's your name?" or "Where do you live?", and so on. But my concern was to discover first in what conditions an answer is valid: it must have a precise bearing on the question asked, which means that the query has been understood; on the other hand, it must furnish the desired information in such a way that this information appears to be well-founded and not at all arbitrary. But, on the other hand, I said, understanding a question is the act of first putting it to oneself, or putting oneself in the mental position of the questioner. Consciousness is the meeting ground of the question and the answer. I would say today, in the light of cybernetics and a host of experiences that have become commonplace, that this should be rectified and defined more precisely. If we think, for example, of the questions which the scientist asks himself about interplanetary space and of the information registered by instruments in satellites we see at once that the example I proposed must be modified. One can definitely not say that the instrument *answers*, any more than the thermometer answers the doctor who wishes to know the temperature of his patient. In every case it is a question of selected elements which lend themselves to a specific reading. It is only from, and as a result of, this reading that there can be an answer, and one might without undue exaggeration even go so far as to say that the questioner is the only one who is in a position to reply, but only at the end of an intermediate process which, needless to say, is extraordinarily complicated.

But the reader will certainly ask what connection there can be between these reflections, which are, in fact, quite elementary, and the problem of man, which, we must not forget, is and must be at the center of this study.

Actually, two connected problems then presented themselves to me: on the one hand, how can what we call *reality*, or, if one prefers, *nature*, answer man in his search for truth? In other words, how can something like the exchange which is established between two human beings talking to one another occur between man and nature? On the other hand— and it is this question on which I wish to dwell at present —how is this dialogue itself, this dialogue between human beings, at all possible? It was from this starting point that I was led to concentrate my attention on the second person who, up to our time, seems to have been so strangely neglected by philosophers. In our time, however, a singular convergence of thought has taken place along this line, undertaken by men working separately and often having no contact with each other. I am thinking primarily of the Austrian Ferdinand Ebner, whose book *Wort und Liebe*,[2] published just before

_____
[2] See *Gesamelte Werke* (Vienna: Thomas Morus Presse, 1952).

the first World War, I did not read until about 1935; but also
of Martin Buber, whose *I and Thou* [3] came to my attention
only long after I had developed my own views on this point.
It could probably be shown that this insistence on the specific
character of the second person is connected with the development of the spirit and method of phenomenology.

And so it was my concern to go to the root of "thou," which
had traditionally been presented to me only as a grammatical
form. One might also say—although I do not believe that I
used the expression at the time—that I had to ask myself what
the grammatical case of the vocative might signify. What happens exactly when I address myself to a human being in order
to . . . ? For the moment I am keeping this row of dots because *in order to* (in French, *pour*) can be defined in very
different ways.

In developing what has previously been said, let us take the
very simple case of my addressing an unknown passer-by in
order to ask him the way. The passer-by is in this case treated
as a pure source of information; one will at first be tempted
to say that there is no great difference between the role thus
assigned him and that of a street map which I consult. Nevertheless this is only an abstract limit. The "thou" here being as
little "thou" as possible, we might express this by saying that
he is not fulfilling the function of an authentic subject (any
more than the street map is). And yet, in reality, it is still a
human being that I am questioning, a being who answers me
in a certain tone of voice, who looks at me in a certain way,
or who perhaps does not even look at me at all; but in this case
I would have the painful impression that he is not treating *me*
as a human being. In this context one thinks of the numberless
employees with whom every one of us is obliged to come in
contact during his lifetime in order to obtain information.
What a happy but rare surprise when the employee is not
content merely with dispensing a mechanical reply, as if he

[3] Translated by R. G. Smith (Edinburgh: Clark, 1952).

were a vending machine, but instead, seems to put himself in
our position to show that he is concerned to help us and, if
he does not possess the information required, to show us where
we might perhaps obtain it ourselves. Examples as commonplace as this are in reality very instructive, for by them we see
how the interlocutor can or cannot behave as a subject—that
is, by treating us (or by not treating us) as subjects ourselves.
But we must not overlook the fact that the term "subject"
here takes on a weight of meaning which it too often lacks
in the usual treatises of philosophy and, especially, of epistemology.

Another example to be found in my *Metaphysical Journal*,
under August 23, 1918, is that of the change which can come
about during a journey in the relationship which develops
between myself and a stranger. To begin with, he may be
only "that skinny little man" or "that short-sighted old man,"
but if the conversation between us, at first entirely commonplace and impersonal, brings us to the discovery of a certain
bond between us, the relationship thus transformed becomes
one of subject to subject. It is curious to note that I only began
to use the indispensable term *intersubjectivity* much later;
and yet it is difficult for me today to understand how I ever
did without it. Certain observations gave me food for thought:
I am thinking above all of the irritation a person invariably
feels when he notes that two others are talking about him
in his presence and calling him "he." ("He is like this," or "He
usually does this," and so on). A person spoken of in this way
feels that he is being treated as an object and so is being rele-
gated to the level of things—or, at best, to the animal level.
He is being deprived of his status as a subject. One might also
say that he feels that he is not *with* ("avec") the others, that
he is being excluded from a certain community to which he
feels he rightly belongs. In such a context the word "with"
appears in a very clear light; but is it really a question of a
relationship? Isn't what we find rather a unity of a supra-

relational kind, like the one that Bradley thought he had discovered in *Feeling?* "It is enough," I wrote, "to reflect on a relationship of the kind that the word *with* suggests to recognize how poor and inadequate our logic is. Apart from juxtapositions pure and simple it is in fact incapable of expressing relationships of an increasing intimacy. If I simply *find myself* in a train compartment or in an airplane *next to* someone to whom I do not speak and whose face *tells me nothing,* I cannot really say that I am *with* him. We are not *together.* I might note in passing that the English noun *togetherness,* which has been unfortunately travestied in popular usage, has no possible equivalent in French. It is as if the French language refused to make a substantive of—that is, to conceptualize— a certain quality of being which is concerned with the '*entrenous,*' the 'between you and me.' "

It was from this time that I began to take seriously such phenomena as telepathy. Suppose, I said, that telepathy exists; in what conditions is it possible? Can it be conceived as the transmission of a message? But first, perhaps, it would be well to reflect on what a message is and under what conditions it can be transmitted. There can be no message of any kind without emission, transmission, and reception. It must, moreover, be added that the term *reception* is inadequate to define an activity which is in reality very complex and which implies a reading or an interpretation. Consider, for example, the case of a person telepathically informed of the death of someone close to him. Manifestly, this could not be conceived as an analogy with the transmission of a message. It would be necessary in fact to admit that the thought of the dying person is endowed with a power of effluence, a phenomenon that is still very obscure and perhaps implies a materializing representation of thought. But it seems as if this supposed emission must be sent out in all directions. How can one conceive that it is "intercepted" by the very person of whom the dying person was thinking, and that the recipient is capable of trans-

lating into sound or visual images the wave so received? Are
not such categories inadequate for something that is rather
of the type of the supra-relational unity which I brought out
by deepening the sense of the very simple word "with"? It
should be noted that other prepositions can likewise come into
play here. I am thinking of *auprès de,* whose equivalent in
English is probably "close to," and of *chez,* which has no exact
English equivalent. These expressions refer to an *intimacy*
which is certainly not the same as the interiority on which
idealists such as Brunschvig laid stress.

It must be said that the metaphysical—today we would more
likely say parapsychological—experiments which I personally
made during the winter of 1916–1917 and which I cannot
retrace here in detail, although they had really disturbing
aspects, convinced me once and for all of the reality of those
phenomena which only ignorance and a willful self-deception
would permit me to doubt. But from this my mind took a path
which in France had not then, I believe, been followed by
anyone, at least by no accredited philosopher, although Berg-
sonian philosophy, to a certain extent, supported similar re-
searches. A note dated April 2, 1916, reproduced here as it was
written, is revealing in this connection:

> I have glimpsed today, on this marvelous clear spring day, that the
> ideas of so-called occult knowledge against which reason attempts
> to rebel are in reality at the root of our most ordinary, most incon-
> trovertible, experiences: experience of the senses, of the will, and of
> the memory. That the will acts as suggestion, let us say as magic sug-
> gestion, who would doubt? And are not bodies, I would not say ap-
> pearances, but apparitions, materializations? And finally, does not the
> experience of memory imply the effective and real negation of time?
> All this is too clear for the half-light of our minds.[4]

This note was written before the experiments to which I
have alluded and, taken word for word, cannot help but raise
objections: I am thinking of the improper use of the word

[4] *Metaphysical Journal,* p. 130.

"occult." But it is of interest as a rendering—though a very clumsy one—of what I would call an anticipatory intuition. By a spontaneous movement of thought, whose origins are perhaps impossible to recover, I categorically rejected the idea, so widely accepted even today, which holds that there are on the one hand normal psychological facts to be taken as "altogether natural" and as explicable to everyone's satisfaction, while, on the other hand, over and above these facts and separated from them by who knows what frontier, there just may be some strange phenomena which could be accounted for at best only by appealing to who knows what forces, or what agents, having nothing at all to do with everyday experience. To this idea my rejoinder was that we probably entertain a number of illusions which must be exposed once and for all. What one affects to consider as obvious—a sensation, a volition, and so on—is in reality no less mysterious than a telepathic phenomenon and is probably not of a very different kind. It is even likely that we must start from the paranormal in order to elucidate the normal—because the very idea of the normal is false, in that it derives exclusively from an entrenched habit of thinking which simply obliterates the fundamental strangeness of the datum.

This is the perspective from which I began to reflect on sensation and to question whether or not sensation could be construed on the usual, if tacitly assumed, model of a message. At the end of the *Metaphysical Journal,* and a little later in the article entitled "Existence et Objectivité," which appeared in 1925,[5] I had already attempted to show that the fact of experiencing a sensation cannot be interpreted as the transmission of something—say, of a wave—which would be incomprehensibly translated or transcribed in such a way as to become what would amount to a psychological state. I took the example of an odor, of a perfume:

[5] *La Revue de Métaphysique et de Morale,* April–June, 1925.

Between the bed of flowers whose perfume comes to me—and my organism—something travels, something is transmitted to me, which the scientist considers as a simple wave of particles. Everyone admits, without asking himself what the hypothesis really means, that this wave, once communicated to the apparatus which it is capable of affecting, is transcribed into olfactory language; however, it remains to be seen whether basically we have a retranscription similar to that which the telegraphist performs on receiving a message, or whether at the source of the wave itself there is not a phenomenon analogous to the phenomenon which takes place in consciousness; in a word, if what I call the flower does not possess an obscure delight in existing which in being communicated to me will become perfume. Admittedly we may be obliged to regard this question as devoid of philosophical meaning. It can be solved—and this in an arbitrary way —only if we suppose that we ourselves make a choice which at bottom is essentially poetical. Moreover, we need to ask ourselves whether there is any meaning whatever in the supposition that a transcription or a translation of the *sensorial message,* from whatever origin it derives, is possible.

Now, by definition, to translate means to substitute one type of *data* for another type of *data,* and for a translation to be possible these data must in some degree be an object for the mind, whereas in the present instance this is inconceivable. For my translating activity to be exercised it must be brought to bear on an *initial datum;* whereas in the case of the hypothesis we have in mind the event that I am supposed to translate into sense-language by very essence is not given to me as datum at all. We are led astray by the crude spatial image from which we cannot escape. We become victims of a confusion between the perturbation communicated *to* our organism and the fact that this commotion is given as datum *to the* subject.[6]

I would express this today by saying that the preposition *to* (à) presents a completely different index in these two cases; it is only in the second that it implies a reference to what I have called intimacy, in whatever register of intimacy that may be.

In the light, not only of my later thoughts, but of those which were to be formulated often much more distinctly by others, and in particular by Heidegger, I would now say that

---

[6] *Metaphysical Journal,* Appendix, pp. 327–328.

what I tried to show was that the fact of experiencing sensa-
tions is in reality a mode of *being in the world*. It must be admitted that these words are a clumsy rendering of the German
expression which has now become familiar—*in der Welt sein*.

The point of this critique will be clearer in the light of the
reflections I was a little later led to develop on the nature of
the relationship between me and my body. It is very important to note that this problem, from a phenomenological point
of view, takes the place of the traditional question of the relationship between soul and body. Attention needs to be focused
on what the simple words "my body" mean. It is very clear
that the possessive "my" cannot be taken here simply in a
possessive sense. The nature of possession, of the act of possessing, is indeed difficult to clarify; so much so that I was
obliged, some ten years later, to sketch out the main lines of a
phenomenology of *having*. When I reflect on my body, I am
naturally inclined to suppose that my body is the instrument
I use in order to perform a certain number of actions, which
make contact with what I shall call exterior reality. But analysis will show that this interpretation—convenient and even
unavoidable though it may be—is philosophically untenable.
In fact, if I ask myself what an instrument is, I find that it is
the extension, artificial or technical, of certain bodily powers.
If I treat these powers as instruments in themselves I find myself involved in an infinite regress. "If I think of my body as
an instrument," I wrote on October 24, 1920, "I attribute to
the soul, of which it would be the instrument, the same po-
tentialities which the instrument would be able to realize. I
furthermore convert the soul into a body and in that way become involved in an infinite regress." [7] Of course it was probably a mistake to fall back on the idea of a soul in formulating
this difficulty. For it is I myself as subject who am trying to
elucidate the relation to this very body, which experience
amply shows I cannot completely control and which some-

[7] *Metaphysical Journal*, p. 246.

times even controls me. But under the massive pressure of experience inseparable from my very self I am obliged to protest with equal firmness against all the tentative efforts I might make to discover an exterior relationship between my body and me: *"I am my body."*

Moreover, one might easily show that this assurance—which I later qualified as existential—is most intimately linked with the assurance I have in the experience of sensing, which rules out thinking of that faculty as a mode of transmission.

Let us beware, on the other hand, of interpreting the affirmation "I am my body" in a materialist sense. Materialism, as such, has no place here. The affirmation only justifies itself inasmuch as my body is de-objectified. What possible sense could there be in saying "I am my body" if my body could be reduced to an extended thing to be exhaustively characterized in terms of objective science? I was even led to introduce the idea of what I called the "body-subject," that is, the body insofar as it is inaccessible to the manipulations, real or ideal, to which the scientist can and must submit extended things. I will say, moreover—at the risk of astounding and even shocking the reader—that in certain instances of healing about which there can be no doubt, we must suppose that healing action is exerted on the body-subject by the action of subject on subject; from this point of view we can understand why it is that one who heals almost invariably begins by placing himself in a state of spiritual readiness, and why the action of healing remains incomprehensible to the healer. I do not wish to dwell here, however, on what for me is only an illustration intended to make a difficult thought a little more intelligible.

But on the other hand I asked myself if this quite singular relationship—it would perhaps be better to say this *nexus*—between my body and me was not at the very heart of what we call existence; if my body as mine, that is to say, taken nonobjectively, might not typify existence. "The world," I said, *"exists* in the measure in which I have relations with it

which are of the same type as my relations with my own body
—that is to say inasmuch as I am *incarnate*." [8] This point is of
some importance; for if I limit myself to regarding the world
as represented (*vorgestellt*) I become incapable of taking into
account its aspect as existing; then the troubling question of
the existence of an external world inevitably arises and in such
a way as to be unanswerable. But to put the question in this
way is precisely to obliterate the very same existential feature
manifest in the union of a subject and a body. In the perspective to which I thus came, the world called "external"
is on the same footing as to its mode of existence with my
body, from which I can only abstract myself by tedious mental
effort.

So one is led to make a fundamental distinction between
existence and objectivity, a distinction which in no way coincides with the one that traditional idealism, particularly since
Kant, makes between subjectivity and objectivity.

Should an attitude of this sort be called realist? Only if we
clearly understand by this an existential realism and not an
objective realism like Perry's which is centered on things as
objects. This is not to question the reality of things but to
specify that their existence is apprehended by incarnate beings
like you and me, and by virtue of our being incarnate. Now
we can begin to see that these reflections have anthropological
import, though the kind of anthropology in question would
be philosophical or existential, not a science concerned with
the objective characteristics and structure of human nature. It
is evident that a philosophy that gives a central importance to
incarnation—and, of course, I am not taking the word in its
theological sense here—will lead to quite a different ethic
from that proposed by a rationalistic idealism which tends to
make the most complete abstraction possible from the concrete
rootedness of human beings. Not that these philosophies necessarily differ in their fundamental intentions, or that they fail

[8] *Metaphysical Journal*, entry of December 3, 1920, p. 269.

to agree at times in their appreciation of certain acts or modes
of human conduct. But I think it would be a serious mistake
to overstate this agreement in order to minimize basic differ-
ences of principle. I remember that more than fifty years ago
a philosopher at the Sorbonne who is today my colleague at
the *Institut* tried to set up a little moral catechism designed
to show that everyone was basically in agreement in judging
this or that act to be licit, illicit, or criminal. I also remember
that as a philosophical neophyte I was profoundly shocked by
such platitudinizing of moral thought. I still believe today
that this reaction was justified. But anticipating a later stage
in my exposition I would now say that many people at the
turn of the century, especially professors of philosophy, were
victims of the strangest illusions concerning the amount of
moral agreement which they imagined firmly established
among civilized men. What a terrible awakening was in store
for these optimists!

The two plays I wrote during the war, *La Quatuor en fa
dièze* and *L'Iconoclaste*, in no way show traces of the events
which I was following from day to day with the liveliest
concern. This is not true, however, of a significant fragment
from a play written by me at that time, with which I shall begin
my next chapter.

On the other hand, *Le Quatuor* and *L'Iconoclaste* do bring
out concretely some of the very personal lines of thought
which I have evoked above. But this in no way means that I
set out to illustrate these thoughts. In each of the plays I
was concerned with certain characters finding themselves in
concrete situations which had been suggested to me in the
one case by a family circumstance which it is unnecessary to
relate here, and in the other by a most extraordinary case
which had been related to me some years before the war by
an Englishman I had met in a hotel in Switzerland.

Claire, the heroine of *Le Quatuor*, is the wife of Stéphane
Mazère, a composer. He pretends to love her, but is not faith-

ful to her, and Claire, driven beyond the limits of endurance, decides to divorce him. Stéphane has a brother, Roger, who loves him deeply, but who also has a great friendship for Claire and continues to see her after the divorce. But Claire seems to be exerting pressure on Roger in order to get him to ask her to marry him. She is, or believes herself to be, in love with him, while he probably has for her only a confused feeling of mingled respect and compassion. They marry.

But Roger, without telling his wife, whom he feels to be hypersensitive and vulnerable, continues to see his brother regularly at their mother's home. They play music together. When Claire discovers that Roger has concealed this persistent intimacy from her she becomes very angry and shows herself inflexible and lacking in understanding. In fact, she personifies moral judgment in its most personal, most restricted, and spiritually most questionable aspect. Roger is mortified by her reaction, which seems petty to him. One wonders whether the marriage will survive this trial.

But then Claire, urged on by a mysterious impulse, conceals herself in the shadows of a concert hall so that she may hear the Quartet in F Sharp which Stéphane has just finished and which is his most personal work. And this quartet, in which Stéphane has transcribed in an immortal way the drama of their life together, and even the memory of their child who died in infancy, gives Claire something like an unsuspected insight, and so she examines herself in the spirit of this music which trancends all jealousies and possessiveness. Can it be that her former love for Stéphane is overtaking her? The truth goes deeper than this. It is as if, through a sort of conversion, but one which has no religious character whatsoever, Claire suddenly had access to a world in which all the categories which revolve around self-love are transcended. And now, for all that she can tell, perhaps what she loved in Roger was a reflection of Stéphane. Once again yielding to an irresistible impulse she admits this discovery to Roger; and the strange thing is that not only is he not resentful but he receives her confession with a sort of gratitude. "You? He?" Claire asks, "What are the borders of a personality? . . . Don't you believe that each of us is extended into everything he cares for?" And Roger murmers, "There is something moving in that thought." Yes, music tells the truth, and music alone. "Perhaps at the bottom of my heart," Roger goes on, "I held it against you that you didn't love Stéphane more." And it seems to Roger that from that moment of authentic meeting their marriage, up to then barren, will perhaps be fruitful.

Here one meets again the primacy of music, which in a certain sense commands the entire development of my thought; but, further, it is obvious that music, or musical consciousness, appears as completely transcending the realm of Eris—that of arguments and disputes in which everyone is revealed as being fundamentally selfish, harboring demands and claims on others. Thus music appears as the sensuous, and at the same time supra-sensuous, expression of that intersubjectivity which opens philosophic reflection to the discovery of the concrete *thou* and *us*. But there is also an intimation here of those reflections on *having* which I was to develop philosophically some ten years later. So, in another instance dramatic vision proves to have been anticipatory, revealing in lightning flashes a terrain later to be explored in discursive thought.

It is the same with *L'Iconoclaste:* Abel Renaudier has been passionately in love with Viviane, the wife of his best friend, Jacques Delorme. But, thinking that Jacques has deserved his happiness, Abel has effaced himself before him and has never come forward to declare his love to Viviane. She dies prematurely. Some time later, during a journey in Russia, Abel learns that Jacques is about to marry again, this time a girl named Madeleine Chazot. Abel is infuriated by what he considers a betrayal pure and simple: and, besides, he considers himself injured. Did not his sacrifice give him the right to think that Jacques would always remain faithful to the mem-

ory of the dead woman? It now seems to him that it is his
duty to avenge her. Jacques no longer seems worthy of keeping unblemished the image of the woman he has rejected by
marrying again. Abel thus resolves to do his utmost to shatter
the image which Jacques has of Viviane: hence the title,
L'Iconoclaste. He tries to make his friend believe that he,
Abel, had once deceived him with Viviane.

But actually he is not fully aware of the conditions under
which the second marriage took place. Jacques was so desperate when his wife died that he seriously considered taking
his own life. But there were his two children whom he had
no right to forsake. On the advice of a friend he undertook
to get into contact with the dead woman through the medium
of automatic writing. A regular communication developed
between them and it was Viviane herself, or so Jacques believed, who begged him to marry Madeleine so that the children would have a second mother. Madeleine, who is a creature of great tenderness and devotion, agreed, fully aware that
Jacques was, or believed he was, in occult communication
with Viviane.

I must say in passing that it is this parapsychological part
of the subject which comes directly from the story I heard
in Switzerland. The man who told me the story was there
with the children of his first wife and with the second who had
just had a child and who appeared completely at ease. I
brooded on what this woman must have felt, involved as she
was in this extraordinary bigamy, and this was one of the
sources of the play, the only one for which I can account.

And so, what Abel took for a betrayal was really a higher
form of faithfulness. In the next scene we see that he has found
a way to sow doubt in Jacques' mind. Madeleine begs him to
give her husband back the peace which his soul has lost. For
she thinks that Jacques might not survive the discovery—that
he has been the victim of an illusion and has perhaps taken
for a real communication what might only be an emanation

from his subconscious; he could think of the relationship only as an illusion if he felt that Viviane had deceived him. Abel, horrified by the consequences of his error, and by the suffering he has created, tries without success to make amends for it. But Jacques no longer believes him. It is in vain that Abel, in order to reassure his friend, puts words into Viviane's mouth, saying that when she was dying she asked him to tell Jacques to marry again after his death. But suddenly Abel feels ashamed of these deceptions. It seems to him that by this kind of intrigue he is desecrating the sanctity of her memory. He feels that he has no choice other than to be absolutely sincere with his friend and he begs him not to hold on to the idea of a wholly precarious and dangerous method of communication, and to accept the mystery which alone can truly reunite. But Jacques himself feels the passionate need of direct contact, of verified contact. He must have a Viviane present to answer him. I will quote here the final speeches of the play, which will be clearer than any commentary.

Jacques (*passionately*). To see, to hear, to touch.

Abel. A temptation which the purest part of you is not deceived by. No, you wouldn't be content in the long run with a world from which mystery has been swept away. Man is like that.

Jacques (*bitterly*). What do you know of man?

Abel. Believe me: knowledge exiles to infinity all that it believes it embraces. Perhaps it is mystery alone which reunites. Without mystery, life would be unbreathable. (*He turns to Madeleine who remains seated, motionless, gazing at nothing.*) And then, you see, one hasn't the right; no, no, one hasn't the right. [He means that one has not the right to maltreat a human being like Madeleine, who through love has agreed to make the greatest sacrifice.]

Madeleine (*imploringly, in a low voice*). Be quiet.

Abel. Ask her forgiveness, humble yourself: there is no other wisdom (*with a sort of sob*). Judges, and iconoclasts—life itself will confound them, life or He who is beyond our words.[9]

Thus, in this ending, in a unique dramatic context, the positive value of mystery is brought to light, as it comes to

[9] *L'Iconoclaste*, p. 47.

be set forth much more explicitly in my later writings. But, fundamentally, Jacques and Abel embody each of the contradictory and seemingly irreconcilable aspects of my thought on the problem of survival, and on the conditions in which we may or may not get in touch with those who have left us and who remain the best of ourselves. We are here at the heart of this questioning thought to which I shall have constantly to return and which is diametrically opposed to a didacticism which I have always abhorred. We should keep in mind this single sentence which anticipates all that I shall have to say later about man today in the dreadful world with which his prodigious feats of technology have confronted him: "You wouldn't be content in the long run with a world from which mystery had been swept away. Man is like that." But must we not ask ourselves, when faced with the dreadful spectacle that we have before our eyes: "Isn't it possible that we might have the power not only to stifle that need but utterly to silence it?"

IV ⤞

Fidelity

Some months ago I reread the fragment I wrote in April
or May 1918, to which I referred in the preceding
chapter. It is the first act of an unpublished play called "Un
Juste" which struck me as having today a significance and even
a premonitional value perhaps greater than the other writings
I have discussed up to now.

It may be best first of all to describe the very special conditions under which the fragment was conceived. It contained,
above all, an unmistakable echo of my thoughts as a civilian
who from the outbreak of the war had been vainly seeking
equilibrium in what was an essentially false position. The
issue was not merely to orient myself with respect to the fighting men, whom I regarded with a feeling of inferiority which
at times bordered on shame, but also to remain true to myself
by not adopting an artificial or fawning attitude toward the
military. At the same time I had to keep from saying in their
presence anything at all which might be a blow to their morale.
But then the problem was how to remain sincere. How was I
to prevent myself from feeling forced into a kind of duplicity,
or even into a lie toward myself?

On the other hand, something had happened the year before which had left a deep impression on me. A school friend
of mine, a dedicated philosopher of great integrity and a

convinced pacifist, had been involved in a case of propagandistic pamphlets sent to the front, after the bloody offensive of April 16, 1917. These pamphlets were undoubtedly calls to revolt, and had much to do with touching off mutinies which occurred in a number of units and which had to be severely suppressed by the commanding officers. A very considerable number of mutineers were turned over to a firing squad.

I had criticized my friend severely for his behavior, and I even wondered how he could endure the thought that he might have contributed to the death sentence of some of the unfortunates whom he had kindled to revolt. At the same time, however, I knew him well enough to realize that his intentions had been very pure and that he had behaved as an idealist. There was in all this a tragic contradiction which kept me thinking for a long time; and such reflection, as so often with me, assumed the form of a drama.

First, it was a question of drawing without the least equivocation as exact a picture as possible of the mentality of the people in the rear of the fighting. In the play, a young soldier, François Lecuyer, has obtained leave after having been awarded the *croix de guerre* for distinguished conduct in battle. Relatives and friends come forward to congratulate him. Among them is an old colonel who in his retirement has been following the detailed account of troop operations in the pages of a large nationalist daily, and who in perfectly good faith recites to himself all the slogans of an optimistic command, condemning as bad citizens those Frenchmen who read the Swiss newspapers in an effort to become acquainted with the enemy's bulletins. Besides the colonel there are the women who want to persuade themselves that their dear soldiers are all cheerful and smiling heroes. But there are also those wives, mothers, and sweethearts who are trembling for their men and wondering in anguish how long the nightmare will last.

There is the cynical shirker, sneering and full of defeatism; but there is also the badly wounded soldier unable to return to the front and to the suffering it entails, while consumed by regret at leaving his comrades. The morale of François, the soldier on leave, is good, but he refuses to ask himself disturbing questions as to the probable duration of the war, the meaning of that war, and what will follow. His brother Raymond, exempted on medical grounds, but trying to make himself useful in every possible way, is, on the other hand, obsessed by these same questions and at the same time feels obliged to keep silent.

But a friend of Raymond's, Bernard Groult, happens to be there too; he is also on leave but he is convinced that he is living his last days and that he will be killed as soon as he returns to the front. He feels that he must communicate to Raymond the nonconformist thoughts he had been mulling over incessantly during nights in the trenches. It is on the questions concerning both the responsibilities and the aims of the war that Bernard finds it impossible to agree with the so-called good Frenchmen—the conformists—of nationalistic circles. This deceitful conformism horrifies him, and he feels that since he has fought in the war he at least has the right to think his own thoughts and to express himself freely before a friend, whereas Raymond does not acknowledge this right as far as he himself is concerned, and suffers from the feeling of being inwardly silenced. As for the young François, he listens to the conversation but is obviously made uncomfortable by it, for it threatens to strike a blow at the morale he wishes to keep intact. Unable to endure such talk any longer, he slips away. Raymond and Bernard remain alone, and the nonconformist soldier no longer hesitates to speak his innermost thoughts. He begins with the origins of the war. Yes, no doubt it was correct on the surface to say that Germany started the war. But behind that Germany there had been a totally criminal Europe. He says:

I can find no trace of clear thinking concerning the inextricable confusion of that last week of July [1914], and it seems to me nobody
wanted what was happening. Everything was ready for the war to
break out. Who touched off the fuse? I know nothing about it, and
I'm not even sure if there is any point in asking such a question.
And even if there had been among them a man, who, in an instant
of criminal lucidity, might have made the decisive gesture, oh well,
I say that it would prove nothing. The deed done, everybody believed himself attacked, and all people were simply defending themselves. And suppose someone dared to set off all this; imagine, if
you please, some metaphysical court before which he would have
to answer. Dared—did we say? Do we know that he did not feel
himself compelled to give the order which was to start everything
going? The act we judge the most free, for all we know, was accompanied by a feeling of the most ineluctable fatality. Which are
we to call right, this immediate feeling or our verdict? And does
the question itself make sense? I picture this man to myself, hounded
by demands, reproaches, and ill-concealed threats. Suppose it was
William II. What is to stop us from believing that he thought it his
duty to forestall a war, and that if he waited a year he would be
committing a crime toward his people? Why couldn't he have believed all that in good faith? And, after all, would he not have been
right if he was convinced that the conflict was inevitable?
Raymond. You know quite well that this is a sophism and that we can
often prevent things from happening simply by postponing them.
Bernard. But if he really was a believer and before God felt responsible for his people, did he have the right to place trust in the favorable prospects which might perhaps have emerged if he had waited?
I imagine him thinking as follows: my duty is to act at any cost.
Perhaps his logic was crude, and I know our conscience repudiates
it, but it was the logic of a prudent ruler who fears God. (*With
vehemence*): Oh, yes, I am as well aware as you that all of this is torture and that it would be better simply to believe like everyone else
that we were faced with a wolf who had attacked a flock of sheep.
Am I to blame if I cannot think so? And does my duty simply consist in plugging up my ears?

The most tragic thing of all is the fact that Bernard, seeing
in the whole conflict nothing but a divided Europe in contradiction with itself, cannot believe in a victory worthy of
the name. What do those people imagine who announce vic-

tory? "A sort of general liquidation. Of what? Of the German people? As if one wiped out an entire nation!" And when
Raymond objects that it is possible at least to obtain a change
of regime and create a new state of mind, Bernard replies only
that such changes cannot be brought about by force.

Only reflection would be of any value. "Let us admit, however monstrous and false the admission, that these atrocities,
the horror of which you can't even suspect, instead of killing
thought and crippling it beyond repair, might some day encourage reflection. But it would be necessary in the event of
that Good Friday, when an enlightened Germany might kneel
in repentance, that she should find herself facing just men."
And that means men who, on the day they have the power,
restrain themselves from trampling underfoot all the fine
principles which they have invoked as long as they found
such principles convenient.

Bernard's words awaken a nameless anguish in Raymond's
heart. If we really stop believing that France is shedding its
blood for true principles, where will our duty lie? The problem seems to him relatively simple for soldiers who have only
to obey. "But the rest of us who have to answer to ourselves,
what about us, Bernard?"

Bernard. My poor fellow, what advice do you expect me to give you?
Raymond. Can you swear to me that in confiding in me you had no
    ulterior motive?
Bernard. Nothing but a fervent and perhaps cowardly need to be
    understood at last. I am so very much alone at the front. Oh, there
    are some good creatures worth you and me put together. But all
    the same . . . And there are those who unknowingly parody us;
    the poor socialist schoolteacher, whom I mentioned to you before,
    with his gentle look behind his spectacles; and then—much worse
    still—the small-town lawyer who plans to engage in left-wing poli-
    tics. They are not the men who will bring peace on earth.
Raymond (who has followed his thought). But is it not treason to
    publish these truths? As you were saying a moment ago, must one
    not risk his life every day in order to have the right to stare such
    truths in the face? And yet, if you who are soldiers think that way,

by what right do the rest of us, who are risking nothing, push this war? Is that not another way to be a traitor and even a more hypocritical and vile one at that?

Bernard. A traitor to what, Raymond?

Raymond. To one's self. One can betray only one's self. All treason is simply a lie. And, do you see—I realize that deep down I have always thought so. The distress I felt in writing to those at the front —the fear of discouraging them, yes—but, above all, the fear of feeding artificially the useful fire of patriotism.

Bernard. Brain fever!

Raymond. I am continually floundering between these two dangers. And now that I have heard you say these frightening things . . . what will happen to me when you are gone?

Bernard (*gently*). Yes.

Raymond. You don't understand: I meant simply when you have gone *back.*

Bernard. No, my dear Raymond, you were right the first time: when I am gone. (*A silence*)

Raymond (*painfully*). But why, if things are really as you say, what good will it do?

Bernard. You are asking what I would be giving my life for. There's that old obsession with the idea of a barter. As if our loftiest experiences didn't become further and further removed from bargaining. A *gift:* think of what that word means in its full strength. If I were to feel even a vestige of regret, I could no longer believe the things I have just told you. The fear that such thoughts express only my personal feelings, unworthy grudges, would poison me. I can express freely and with certainty the complete horror which this war inspires in me only because I have accepted once and for all my share of whatever atrocities the war may bring upon me. Oh, there are times when I imagine things and when I tremble. But lucid thought comes to one only on acceptance of complete sacrifice. Such thought is translucent through and through; it is incarnate in sacrifice, as the soul is in the body. It has not been given to me in exchange for something else.

Raymond. And yet this thought has nothing in it which could enable one to live; it reveals error and death everywhere.

Bernard. How is it then that the look on your face is no longer the same since you have understood me? What does it matter if this thought, in me who will die tomorrow, is only a conscious and purified resignation, if in you it can become translated into action?

"Peace to men of good will" is the usual bad translation. It should be: "Let peace be wrought *by* men of good will" (*a long silence*). *Raymond* (*in a low voice*). Would *that* then be my duty?

In the acts to follow, which were never written, Raymond was to become involved in a pacifist action, like that friend of mine whom I mentioned earlier; probably at the end, horrified by the consequences that his act would have entailed, he would have reopened the whole question or perhaps killed himself.

Although the reasons for my not completing this play were not then apparent, they are plain enough to me now. Apart from the fact that I did not feel myself adequate to portray a military setting which I knew only through books or reports I had heard, the sequence of action, dramatic as it might be, no longer interested me. There was the risk of its developing almost mechanically. The essential aspect of the case for me lay in the initial tie between Bernard and Raymond.

If it appears that I have given too much emphasis to this fragment, I may point out that the problem posed there is the very one which was to arise again later, particularly in the Algerian situation, for example, when a number of well-known intellectuals published a manifesto in favor of insubordination; the question arose then, and pointedly, as to whether these men were behaving like traitors or not. But in terms of my own philosophical perspective I should emphasize that it was in that rough draft of the play and in reference to a very concrete situation that the problem of fidelity first appeared to me—a problem which was subsequently to assume for me so important a philosophical role. Now it is interesting to note that in this instance, as so often, dramatic creation anticipated reflective thought.

Actually it is natural that it should be so, since reflection always comes after experience. But here we are concerned with a very special type of experience embodied in imaginary people in conflict with one another. The word "imaginary" might cause misunderstanding. More precisely, it would be important to introduce a distinction between the characters who imposed themselves on me with as much force as if I had met them in actual life, and those whom I had invented, for example, because I needed them to advance the action but who were in fact only a means and had no value of their own. Perhaps only these invented characters should be called "imaginary." I should note in this regard that in the so-called "pièce à thèse," or philosophical play, a type of drama I have always detested for this very reason, the characters are invariably made up in order to illustrate ideas or to serve as a foil for those characters who illustrate them.

If my own plays were of this type, I would have carefully abstained from giving them so important a place in these lectures, since they would add precious little to the philosophical writings themselves. But in fact the contrary is true. I should be tempted to say that these characters were formed out of my own substance in accordance with a process perhaps not very different from those studied by biologists. I must also add that the words "my own substance" correspond to something quite mysterious, something which in no way coincides with what might be either the life I have actually lived or the characteristics manifested by that life. As Ariadne, the heroine of my *Chemin de crête*, says: "The most terrible thing in life is that the possessions of which we have been deprived are not only missing, but they exist in us like upside-down shadows, nocturnal and devastating powers." In other words, in a very profound sense, *we are also what we are not*; there is a counter-reality to ourselves which is not embodied directly in our acts, but which may hover over them like a shadow, and I would not hesitate to say that for the novelist or playwright this counter-reality may become the source of creation itself. Moreover, in my own experience I have found that fictional characters can take shape only within a specific situation where they have to confront one another and which I

would compare to the harmonic setting in music, within which
a melodic theme is developed; for the melody never presents
itself out of the blue, ready for any sort of harmonic setting.
It is, rather, born into a particular setting—as characters into
a particular situation.

I am fully aware of the disconcerting nature of such considerations for the reader who would probably—and quite
understandably—expect a professional philosopher to develop
ideas according to the usual deductive or nondeductive, dialectic or nondialectic, modes of reasoning. But I have emphasized from the beginning that what I am trying to present
here is not so much a formal treatise, but rather an inquiry
which attempts to reflect on its own development. Furthermore, this inquiry is oriented toward the immediate problems
which a man must face if he wants to ask himself about the
future of human reality in today's world, and about the resources which may still be available if there is to be any escape
from a fate which no longer appears to us as external but
which seems to issue directly from human reality.

Just after the first World War, while I was at Sens as a
teacher of philosophy, I wrote a large number of plays which
seemed to me then to be entirely independent of my philosophical work; in fact, it seemed for a while that the plays might
even take the place of my other writings. I am thinking, for
example, of *Le Regard neuf, Le Mort de demain, Le Cœur
des autres,* and even of my *Un Homme de Dieu* and of *La
Chapelle ardente.* It was only later that I understood that this
separation was illusory, and that through all the plays I was
pursuing the same inquiry which was to become embodied in
the philosophical writings composed ten or fifteen years later.

But it seems almost as if it had been necessary for the reflective work to be postponed, for if it had been effected prematurely it would doubtless have struck a blow at the autonomous reality and immediacy of the characters who imposed
themselves on me in the various dramatic works. I shall come

back to two of these plays later on. But first I would like to return to the problem posed in "A Just Man" in an attempt to show how the draft of the play anticipates an existential way of thinking long before the more conscious formulation of it on my part, and the more systematic development of it, in a direction quite different from mine, by Sartre.

Here exactly is what I mean to point out: we can no longer simply ask ourselves whether Bernard's conclusions were right or wrong. We have to make more subtle distinctions here. Bernard, as we can see clearly today, is not mistaken when he speaks of a Europe at war with itself. The future was more than to confirm his fears. The second World War consummated the suicide of Europe, and all the events which now unfold before our eyes at an accelerated pace are simply the consequences of that suicide. But the important question is a different one; it belongs to the realm of ethics. It is concerned with whether Bernard does or does not have the right to pronounce before another person a judgment which is going to have a profound effect upon that person's conduct. Nothing is more significant than the sentence in which he says that if he had not accepted what he thought was the worst for himself, he could not have conceded himself that right. This amounts to saying that what justifies not the judgment but the articulation of that judgment—that is, its place in existence —is a certain value which is itself existential. Traditional philosophy has accustomed us to thinking otherwise by laying down as a principle that a truth is in no way affected by the situation in which the person who states it is placed. I was to express this thought much later by saying that the ontological weight of a statement implies something more than the content of that statement. Thus, for example, I was to reproach Sartre, when he came to Geneva in 1946, for having welcomed the journalists who came and greeted him by telling them, "Gentlemen, God is dead." I said: "If one sticks to the content, that is, to the statement, it is the same as Nietzsche's, but in reality it is not the same phrase because the existential context is quite different. In Nietzsche this terrible affirmation is a private thought uttered in fear and trembling by a thinker who feels himself condemned to sacrilege; put forth by Sartre at the airport it becomes a headline for the dailies and is by that very fact devoid of its substance."

Bernard speaks like a man who knows, or thinks he knows, that he is going to die and can believe himself morally compelled to delegate to the one who is going to survive a mission which circumstances have not allowed him to carry out, so that he judges himself as in error or even guilty for that failure. What is certain in any case is that Raymond and, to a lesser degree, Bernard, are animated by the same will to be faithful, the same deep fear of treason, but without knowing what or to whom one must be faithful. What does it mean not to be a traitor?

What I now have to show is how, starting from a date that I can no longer fix absolutely, but which must have been around 1930 or a little before, this theme of fidelity assumed a central importance for me, as is shown by the following un-dated note from *Being and Having:* "Being as the place of fidelity." And I added: "How is it that this formula arising in my mind at a given moment of time has for me the inex-haustible inspiration of a musical theme?——Access to Ontol-ogy.—Betrayal as an intrinsic evil." [1]

There is certainly room for believing that this sentence struck me after my conversion to Catholicism in 1929. But this conversion, on which I do not have to dwell here since it belongs to a dimension other than that of our present in-quiry, did not appear as a break but rather as the accomplish-ment and almost the conclusion of thoughts which had been developing in me for more than ten years. The question that had been posed to me by François Mauriac in a letter of

[1] *Being and Having,* trans. Katherine Farrer (Westminster, Dacre Press, 1949). Quotations from this work are from the English edition.

thanks for the article I had devoted to one of his books, "Why don't you rejoin us?", consolidated a resolve in me. Whether this resolve would have arisen spontaneously or not I shall never know. But what is certain is that its crystallization had been prepared by the deep friendship which bound me to the critic Charles Du Bos, who, though a Catholic by birth, had only just rediscovered his own religion at a depth to which he had never before had access. How can I fail to underline the role of these friendships and such meetings as these in my life? These encounters always appear in retrospect as having been called for from within my very self so that in such a domain the distinction between external and internal ultimately becomes irrelevant, or, more exactly, becomes absorbed into an harmonically richer reality. It seems to me that these encounters which enrich the very texture of our lives can be understood by analogy with what happens in musical creation where one theme calls forth another.

If now I ask myself about the enlightening force of those words, "Being as the place of fidelity," I would say that a purely psychological interpretation which would bring out the role that attachments to parents and friends played in my life is quite inadequate here and even misses the essential point. It would be appropriate, however, to fathom the meaning of these words which, taken literally, may well arouse objections. These words only seem to assume meaning through some such mediating idea as that of "light." It would be proper, moreover, to substitute a verb for the noun and also to have recourse to a dynamic terminology rather than a language that is too static. We thus end up with formulas such as the following: to live in the light of fidelity is to move in the direction of Being itself. But we still have not eliminated the noun, Being. Now it is very clear that there would be no sense in conjuring up Being as some sort of terminus which we would be approaching. On the contrary, we can certainly conceive the possibility of a sort of hierarchy among modes of Being so that it would then be possible *to be* more or less fully. We may then understand how one who is faithful would actually be on the way to being more fully in contrast to one who dissipates himself in conflicting feelings and incoherent actions.

All of this, however, could take on meaning only if we proceed to a scrupulous examination of fidelity, and this examination should bring out the necessity of our looking upon genuine fidelity as creative in contrast to those who see in fidelity something like an inertia of the soul. This confusion has been indulged and sanctioned in a kind of literature whose principal representative in France has been André Gide. For the author of *Nourritures terrestres*, value is tied up with the perpetual siege of novelty and with the refusal to let one's self be burdened by a past devoid of life. For my own part, I have always been on the scent of novelty in every domain— no doubt to excess—but at the same time I have always been on guard against this too simple fashion of conceiving our attitude with respect to duration and more exactly with respect to creatures who endure.

If I am not mistaken, the expression, "creative fidelity," appears for the first time in my essay entitled "On the Ontological Mystery," which is at the center of my philosophical work:

> Fidelity is actually the exact opposite of an inert conformism. It is the active recognition of something abiding, not formally—in the manner of a law—but ontologically. In this sense fidelity is always bound up with a presence, or even with something that can and should be upheld in us and before us as a presence, but which, *ipso facto*, can be just as well ignored, forgotten, obliterated—even utterly so; and this may remind us of that shadow of betrayal which, to my mind, threatens to envelop our entire human world.[2]

Thus the connection between fidelity and presence is affirmed with the greatest possible clarity. We meet here for the first time in these lectures the term *presence*, which occurs

[2] *Philosophy of Existence.*

so often in my writings; but we must admit that it is certainly impossible to give a rigorous definition of it. Presence can only be—not grasped, for that would be contradictory—but evoked through the aid of direct and unchallengeable experiences which do not rise from the conceptual apparatus which we make use of in order to reach objects. We know only too well how easy it is for each of us to find himself with others who are not significantly present at all. And, strangely enough, this can appear the more clearly the more we know about them in a practical way—for example, when we know in advance just how they will react, as if automatically, to whatever we may say. We return here to what has been said previously on the subject of the *thou* and of the relation designated by the word *with*. Let us recall, for example, in order to see all of this more concretely, the sort of experiences we all may have had in connection with a funeral. Certain persons whom we would consider perhaps as friends have offered us only stereotyped formulas which seem to be delivered by an automatic distributor; those persons were not present and we ourselves were not present for them. Some other person, on the contrary, by a look, an intonation, or by the very quality of his silence, has brought us an undeniable testimony of presence. We were together, and this encounter, this co-presence, has left behind a sort of furrow which prolongs it. Each of us, if he really wishes to take the trouble to go ahead with this sort of discrimination, will come to recognize that there are presences and loyalties in his life which differ radically from worldly or professional relations and the obligations which issue from them.

Here we have a kind of evidence which differs, as much as anything could, from Cartesian evidence, that is, from the evidence associated with clear and distinct ideas. Must we go so far as to say that it is a purely private and incommunicable evidence which exists for me alone? I do not think so. I rather think that in this case, as in many others, perhaps chiefly in the domain of art, we have to interpose, if I may put it that way, an intermediary kind of given between that which is accessible to just anybody on the one hand, and that which I alone am able to appreciate on the other: this intermediary given is for a concrete *us;* it is an open communion of selves, the kind which is formed around a work that is intimately loved but which we know will remain a closed book for an infinity of creatures.

These reflections make it possible for us to see very distinctly, I think, why it is so difficult to *speak* of presence; it is because through this speech we inevitably transform and degrade presence. In order to realize this we need only think of the kind of betrayal which so often occurs in commemorative speeches. It is as if these speeches only contributed to obscuring the person in whose honor they are given; for that incommunicable essence to which we have vowed our fidelity they substitute images or ideas which have virtually nothing in common with it.

An objection is almost certain to arise here and it would be well to deal with it directly: do we not usually speak of fidelity to a cause or to a principle? But then what becomes of presence as we have been defining it? I believe we must reply that there may well be some continuity between the fidelity which we have been discussing and those attachments which may, after all, be nothing more than modes of inertia or laziness, a laziness which here amounts to blind obstinacy. But in this case, as in so many others, thought has the obligation, it seems to me, to reascend this incline of degradation and to reawaken in us in some manner the memory of those pure experiences charged with Being which habit and the tasks of daily life seem joined in a conspiracy to make us forget.

It would be of some interest to refer here to the profound views of Royce on loyalty. He is to be credited with realizing very clearly the supra-personal character of the cause to which the loyal soul dedicates himself. But this means that the cause in this sense can never be reduced to a mere abstract principle —for example, that of justice. It is always necessary that some concrete context enter into fidelity, and I should like to be able to call this context "présentiel," if this term were admitted in philosophical discourse as the term "existential" now is.

But it was in quite a different perspective, it seems to me, from that of the Roycian account that I first approached, in 1932, a problem which since that date has constantly preoccupied me and which, moreover, arises in some manner in any involvement whatever. It comes up the moment the climate of a certain sincerity, understood as accord with one's self in *the immediate*, is assumed. It is no doubt superfluous to recall how avidly a writer like André Gide has championed this sort of sincerity.

The very simple example to which I refer in *Being and Having* [3] is that of a promise made—no doubt on the spur of the moment—to a sick person whom one has seen in the hospital where he is laid up with an incurable disease. As I so often do, I resorted to the personal form: seized with pity at the sight of the sick person, moved by discovering that my visit caused him an unexpected joy, I promise to come to see him often. This promise is made on the basis of a certain disposition within me. A few days pass. I notice with some embarrassment that although the sick person's condition is not improved, my disposition is no longer the same. A strange remoteness has replaced the sincere and immediate sympathy that I had felt while with him. Now I think of him only abstractly. I am going to have to return and visit him since I promised to do so, but the visit now assumes a merely burdensome aspect. And I asked myself: in making this promise I took it for granted, it seems—and implicitly had the understanding if only with myself—that my inner attitude would remain the same. But now that I see how poorly I knew my-

[3] Page 47f.

self, by what right can I make this sort of draft on the future? Or else must I think that by assuming this engagement I was telling myself: even though I shall no longer experience a few days from now the feeling which at this moment dictates my promise, I shall behave as though I were feeling the same way. For, after all, I have no right to make this unfortunate man suffer the unpredictable fluctuations in my way of feeling. However, in this case would I not be condemning myself to playing a farce by pretending to feel what I no longer feel? Here we have, I may say parenthetically, the theme of the heart's fluctuations, so masterfully elaborated by Proust.

The example I have given is a relatively trivial one. Furthermore, I may well be told, reassuringly, that though I may leave my home halfheartedly to make the visit, regarding it as a chore to be done, there is always the possibility that when I arrive in the presence of the sick man, my initial feeling of compassion may come over me again.

But is it not clear that these data recur in the same fashion in the vastly more serious case of a promise of marriage? In an exalted moment and surely under the influence of a great many facts of a nonobjective sort, such as the effects of the hour, the surroundings, the landscape, and so on, a young man suddenly proposes to a young lady whom he had perhaps not contemplated marrying. His proposal is accepted, and there he is tied by his promise. What is important to notice here is that in cases like this the obscure and unspecifiable conditions which prefaced the proposal and the subsequent involvement are scarcely taken into account, and it is even less likely that any mention will be made of them between the persons involved. How, then, can we dream of making the validity of the promise depend on the persistence of the more or less determining conditions under which the promise was made? Everything happens, then, as though these conditions had no bearing whatsoever on the matter. Besides, it is not even proper to speak of a judgment here, since that would require the conditions to be specified like a bill of particulars, which is hardly conceivable. What is in fact produced is a decision: *I shall treat these conditions whatever they may be as negligible.* Very probably in most cases this decision is not in itself a consciously made decree; let us say rather that everything happens as though the promise were unconditionally binding. It goes without saying that neither would say to the other that such a voluntary decree had been taken. It appears certain to me that in this sort of situation this type of analysis, to which a third unprejudiced party would judge it advisable to proceed, will not occur, or, if it does, it would occur only later and too late at that. Rather it seems that everything happens as though the moment of exaltation I mentioned before was asserting itself like an indissoluble absolute, confident of its perpetuity.

It seems superfluous to repeat in connection with this example everything I have said on the subject of the preceding one. But obviously the problem of the marriage proposal is vastly more serious than the visit promised to the sick man and considerably complicated by the fact that commitment is mutual.

But how avoid inferring from all this that an unconditional commitment—that is, one in which those involved more or less explicitly refuse to consider as relevant conditions which obscurely but certainly contributed to it—is an essentially dishonest act, or even one that arises from a sort of romanticism which deliberately fails to acknowledge the structural facts of experience.

Following out this line of thought, which is that of critical judgment, or, if you like, of understanding, one might easily maintain that only promises of limited duration would meet the requirements of a mind concerned to be honest; such promises might be renewed of course but only by common consent. Naturally, even in such commitments unspecified factors would still intervene but the evil would not be great since possibilities of escape more or less comparable to safety-valves would have been arranged at the outset. We might readily admit that this would only be a compromise, but it would surely be the lesser evil, for to rule out all commitment would be to instate anarchy pure and simple in human relations.

Nevertheless, it seems to me that something in us protests in a more or less inarticulate fashion against this radical elimination of unconditional commitment. Should we say that we are dealing here simply with a case of a simple anachronism and that its sacred character is precisely what ought to be considered antiquated?

But here we are encountering a type of assertion which is becoming increasingly fashionable in our times and which we find it important to subject to rigorous examination. It consists in judging that for contemporary man such an unconditional way of being or of belief is no longer necessary. Even some theologians have not been exempt from contamination by this odd historicism; I am thinking in particular of the rationalism underlying, it seems to me, the thinking of Bultmann. "No man today," he says, "can believe any longer in a miracle."

Surely those who express such thoughts must be aware that in fact there exist men, perhaps even in great numbers, who do not seem to suspect any such incompatibility between their belief and the requirements, set up as normative, for modern man. But this fact could be met by treating that anachronistic mentality as a fossil—as if one were dealing with individuals who did not know they belonged to historical layers covered over by later sedimentations.

For my part, however, I would say that we should denounce right now the illusion associated with this type of assertion. In fact we should survey with the greatest care the fields in which the word "antiquated" may properly be used. This is the case in the scientific field insofar as certain theories or hypotheses really seem to have been definitively refuted or superseded. I say "seems" because it is possible that an idea once believed to be absolutely and forever obsolete may reappear in a renovated form. Nonetheless we may, despite this reservation, accept in principle the fact that in the positive sciences, and even more so in the technological sciences, we are confronted with genuine irreversibility.

We may be tempted perhaps to say the same, though in a very different sense, for customs, mores, and institutions. Yet it would be necessary, if we take history into account, to introduce many fine distinctions; revolutionary upsets may always occur to belie for an indeterminate time any assertion that "it is no longer possible today . . ." One need only remember, for example, what has happened in certain people's democracies, such as Czechoslovakia.

Nevertheless an exception must certainly be made—and we shall see why more and more clearly—of the field in which freedom reigns sovereign, the domain of love and, I would add, of faith. But what comes in and confuses everything here is the devaluation in everyday usage of such words as love and faith; and it must be noted as an agonizing paradox that it is exactly on words designating the highest realities that this devaluation—I might even say degradation—is most widely exercised.

From what I have said there is every reason to view with the greatest distrust the presumption of those who dare to assert, for example, the disappearance of the sacred.

It is appropriate at this point to introduce an essential distinction: It is easy to see how in the world around us the process of abolishing the sacred is accomplished and is accelerated, and it is not difficult for us to imagine that here or there a state of things could be established so that the very meaning of the word sacred would no longer be understood by anyone. But this by no means signifies that, judged from the standpoint of reflective thought, this obliteration *de facto* of the sacred corresponds to a refutation *de jure*. Everything seems to indicate that this radical profanation could not be accomplished without striking a blow at what are probably unformulated needs which are deeply inscribed in the very heart of a human being. Eventually I shall have to return to this problem, which is an extremely acute one in the world today. But I could not speak of unconditional commitment without at least mentioning it.

What must also be brought to light is the fact that love, in the fullest and most concrete sense of the word, namely, the love of one being for another, seems to rest on the unconditional: *I shall continue to love you no matter what happens.* This is at the very opposite pole from the conditional commitment which seems to presuppose a *de facto* if not a *de jure* stability only under the limited circumstances in which it is made. We should also say that love, far from merely requiring the acceptance of risk, demands it in a certain manner; love seems to be calling for a challenge to be tested because it is sure to emerge the conqueror.

When I refer back to those "Notes" of 1932 which figure in *Being and Having* and to the "Meditation" of 1933 for which they were prepared, I find that at that time I did not place so much stress on risk. My fundamental preoccupation is expressed rather by the simple formula which will be the starting point of my next chapter: *the necessity of restoring to human experience its ontological weight.* It would hardly be wrong to say, it seems to me, that in these few words, whose meaning needs to be elucidated, the program for all my later investigations was expressed.

V ⤙

The Ontological Mystery

I CANNOT overlook the disconcerting character that the end of the preceding chapter may have had for some of my readers. This may have been due simply to the still far too indistinct way in which the inquiries concerning human relations and their possible evaluation were intermingled with strictly metaphysical investigations. The programmatic formula on which I ended, "the necessity of restoring to human experience its ontological weight," compels me, by the very fact of its obscurity, to make an indispensable clarification.

Such a formula expresses a very particular sort of insight. I say "insight," *not* intuition, because this latter term has been used by philosophers, especially in our time, in senses too diverse and sometimes even too poorly defined to permit our using it without equivocation. In truth, it is the Greek word *syneidesis* which appears to me to be the most adequate. As the etymology of the word suggests, what is meant is a kind of vision which brings things together and which, precisely for that reason, implies a prior development. But at the same time it seems to me that this *syneidesis* must subsequently prompt us to an intellectual task which consists first in scrutinizing its sense or value. If I consider in an objective manner the words "the ontological weight of human experience" their meaning is certainly not manifest and, conceivably, to some of my readers they might seem literally meaningless.

In order to clarify this formula, it is certainly proper to begin with the fact that what a person says may have weight or not, but obviously we are dealing with a quality that can be appreciated, but not measured, as it is literally unquantifiable. Let us try to be more precise and remember that what a person says embodies a suggestion formulated in a definite context, and in a context perhaps capable of orienting my behavior. To say that the suggestion has weight appears to indicate that it has been duly thought out and is in direct contrast, for instance, to a suggestion given lightly and impulsively. The latter incorporates no guarantee of any sort. But between the weight and the warrant of an assertion there exists a definite connection. If this suggestion has weight for me, it is because it was given to me by someone whom I have every reason to trust. One might even add that the weight is not separable from a certain substance—I might even call it a certain density—which corresponds to an abundance of motivation, completely absent in one who speaks without rhyme or reason.

These introductory remarks at least have the value of bringing certain matters into focus, as one does with an optical instrument.

But what does ontological weight mean here? In another note dating from about the same time, I spoke of an ontological stake. Let us note that I was not taking account of the distinction made by Heidegger between ontic and ontological. Ontological weight means the weight of Being or weight with respect to Being. But it is necessary to add immediately that all this is absolutely incomprehensible if one includes in the meaning of the word *Being* anything that might be compared to an object. We observe in passing that the English language does not permit drawing a distinction between *Sein* and *Seiendes*, which at least can be translated into French. But it seems to me indispensable to underline the fact that the Being which is meant in such expressions as ontological weight or stake must be understood as a verb and *not* as a noun. And when I look back at all these 1932 texts, I am tempted to think that on this point I have not always been explicit enough. For instance, in the "Meditation" of 1933, to which all these notes were precursors, I said that Being is that which resists or would resist a reductive analysis bearing on the immediate data of experience. The danger that such a formulation presents is that it seems to interpret Being as residual. The difficulty in all this stems from the fact which Bergson to his great credit emphasized so unremittingly, that human language seems indeed to be modeled on things.

We would be closer to the truth if we said that the irreducibility affirmed in that formula belongs to an experience on which critical analysis has not and cannot have any hold, short of substituting for the experience something else, something that it is not. Nevertheless, this formula is still unsatisfactory. To assimilate Being to a mode of experience is to fall into the pitfalls of psychology and psychologism. It would not be wrong to say, in a perspective quite similar to that of Fénelon, that we human beings are a species "in-between," between Being and Non-Being, or even that we are called upon to *be* —that it is our responsibility to *be*. What begins to emerge here is the plenitude to which we aspire. Yet here again the language is deceptive. It could, in effect, cause us to think of Being as an ideal. But, precisely, between Being and the ideal there is a radical opposition. And we could return here to what was said in an earlier chapter about "participation." But as I have already explained, this term "participation," although used systematically by a thinker like Louis Lavelle, is itself definitely subject to caution insofar as it seems to invoke a part-whole distinction. Now the plenitude in question cannot in any way be identified with a totality susceptible of being divided or fragmented.

We could, on the other hand, help forward the course of thought as much as possible in the direction of Being by referring to a concrete totality such as an orchestra performing a polyphonic work. Each performer indeed plays his part in the ensemble; but it would be absurd to identify this ensemble with an arithmetical sum of juxtaposed elements. We should completely misunderstand what a musical ensemble really is. But we can very well imagine the process of thought in the course of which the instrumentalist, who in the beginning was conscious only of the part which had been entrusted to him—if only because he had had to work on that part separately at first—little by little becomes consciously aware of the ensemble. And it is probable that by that very fact the interpretation of his own part will be transformed. It is obvious that this concrete whole, namely, the performance of the polyphonic work, cannot be likened to an ideal. From the viewpoint of the composer each part could only be conceived as a function of the whole. The whole precedes the parts, as many philosophers, especially Kant, have shown in the case of living organisms.

Here we have a comparison which is enlightening, at least to a certain point. But we must admit that nothing permits us to assert that each individual's experience can be compared to a part in a symphony. The symphony presupposes the composer who has thought it through as well as the orchestra leader in whom or by whom this composer's thought is actualized. But it would be falling again into a precritical dogmatism, it seems to me, to claim from my experience alone, with its gaps and its insufficiencies, that I am obliged to go back to the existence of an all-inclusive thought which controls it. It would be hardly less arbitrary, moreover, to deny a priori the existence of such a thought. In other words, ever since I have begun to think for myself, I have never ceased to protest just as much against an absolute idealism (considered preferably in the terms of the Anglo-Saxon neo-Hegelians) as against those philosophies which have dogmatically taken the opposite stand. Here I have in mind certain pluralists at the beginning of the century.

But what we have to become aware of, short of any adherence to such doctrines, is that any human experience lends itself to an internal transformation somewhat comparable to that I alluded to apropos the instrumentalist. And what may be even more important is that each of us this very day may meet another human being who will appear to be much farther ahead than any of us along that way of which we can see only the beginning, as when we seek our way in a fog. Once again, let me adopt the personal form of expression: this person presents himself to me as a witness. He attests by his presence to that mode of being toward which I am groping and trying to carry with me all those who are close to me. But what in fact is being attested in this manner? What is disclosed to me is that this *other* person bears in himself a certain life and that he radiates this life like a light. And from the moment that I benefit from this attestation it may well be that I aspire to become a co-witness with this other being. The characteristics of this life considered in its increasing dynamism will appear more clearly in what follows, but what we can say now, in order to avoid an indeterminacy comparable to a rarified atmosphere in which thought cannot live, is that this life is inseparable from love.

If we return to the initial formulation, the elucidation of which was our task, we may say, although it is still only a tentative approximation, that what I have called the ontological weight of human experience is the love which it is able to bestow.

But here again we must be careful not to succumb to the temptation to psychologize. And here it is essential to invoke the distinction between problem and mystery which suddenly forced itself upon me in the winter of 1932. This distinction also was revealed to me in a flash of insight, a *syneidesis*, with-

out my being able to reconstruct completely the process of
thought which led me to it. It was while I was taking a walk
in Paris that the insight suddenly came over me. Unfortunately
this distinction has been overused by the popularizers and
their books, and it has become a sort of philosophical commonplace, losing thereby the original and challenging character which it had initially. I believe I must cite here the few
lines from *Being and Having* where this sort of insight is re-
corded:

October 22nd

The Position of the Ontological Mystery: Its Concrete Approaches.

This is the proposed title for my paper to the Marseilles Philosophical Society. The phrase 'mystery of being, ontological mystery' as
against 'problem of being, ontological problem,' has suddenly come
to me in these last few days. It has enlightened me.

Metaphysical thought—reflection trained on mystery.

But it is an essential part of a mystery that it should be acknowledged; metaphysical reflection presupposes this acknowledgment,
which is outside its own sphere.

Distinguish between the Mysterious and the Problematic. A problem is something met with which bars my passage. It is before me in
its entirety. A mystery, on the other hand, is something in which I
find myself caught up, and whose essence is therefore not to be before
me in its entirety. It is as though in this province the distinction between *in me* and *before me* loses its meaning.[1]

I shall end the quotation at this point, but not without not-
ing that I allude a little later on to the fact that Maritain had
already recognized that there is a mystery of knowledge which
is of the ontological order. Specifically, this view is expounded
in *Réflexions sur l'intelligence*,[2] the only work of the Thomist
philosopher, it seems to me, that made a strong impression
on me; and indeed it may be that it was through this book that
I was led to make the fundamental distinction I am discussing

[1] *Being and Having*, p. 100.
[2] Jacques Maritain, *Réflexions sur l'intelligence et sur sa vie propre* (Paris:
Desclée, de Brouwer, 1931).

here. As in another instance—I have in mind particularly
Schelling's distinction between negative and positive philosophy—it is possible that the progression of thought was pro-
moted by a misconception and that I had understood by the
words "mystery of knowledge" something which was in itself
quite foreign to Maritain's thought. I might note in passing
that we saw each other continuously during a winter spent
in Versailles, at the home of our mutual friend, Charles Du
Bos. What Maritain tried to do was to instruct both of us in
certain aspects of Thomist doctrine, but, as a matter of fact,
neither Charles Du Bos nor I was converted by any manner
of means to this type of thought.

To tell the truth, I am not certain that the term "mystery"
—for which I can find no equivalent that satisfies me—has
not helped maintain a somewhat regrettable confusion; "mystery," at least removed from its theological context, is hardly
separable from certain associations from which it *should* be
completely dissociated. When a writer of detective novels,
for example, entitles one of his books *The Mystery of the
Yellow Room*, he is telling us implicitly that he will proceed
to the elucidation of a certain affair which, at the outset, is
presented as obscure and perplexing. Here the skill of the
author is exercised at the beginning of his story by rendering
this obscurity as impenetrable as possible. The mystery continues to exist for us as long as the key to the enigma has not
been revealed. We are *a priori* certain, when we begin to read
the novel, both that the solution exists and that it will be disclosed to us at the end of the story. It is the structural condition of this genre of literature.

But what should strike us immediately in speaking of the
mystery of Being is that in this case some mystery of an entirely different sort is meant. If we viewed this matter from
the perspective of a certain kind of agnosticism which was
widespread in the nineteenth century (but which appears
today to be somewhat out of fashion), we would be tempted

to speak of an insoluble problem—that is, a problem which does not allow of a solution. It seems to me, however, that philosophers today would be quite willing to admit that, taking all things into account, a problem which does not allow of a solution is no doubt a problem that has been badly posed (I recognize, however, that one could argue this point). But what is certain is that the word "mystery" is used in *Being and Having* and in all my subsequent writings in an absolutely different sense. The word applies to what cannot be conceived as a problem, to what is repugnant to problematizing. Clearly, we link up here with what in the *Metaphysical Journal*, some ten years before, I had called the "non-mediatizable immediate," [3] as opposed to the common or everyday immediate which, unlike the former, gives rise to an indefinite number of mediations. What must be stressed above all is that the mysterious evoked here must be looked for in the direction of light rather than in the direction of obscurity. Whatever is obscure is, in effect, for the mind the initial phase of a certain elucidation; and, inversely, no elucidation is possible except in regard to a datum which is relatively obscure. The highly varied and complex operations studied by epistemology appear upon reflection as ideal manipulations carried out on data which have themselves been produced by previous elaboration.

But reflection shows that our experience is by no means reducible to such schema and that it is very far from lending itself to an unlimited problematizing. We could say further that all problematizing is accomplished on the basis of that which in itself is not capable of being problematized. I have often stressed the limitations which attend all optical representations of knowing. In an excellent article in *Commonweal* on my style of thought, Mr. Seymour Cain observed correctly that I am not a spectator who is looking for a world of structures susceptible of being viewed clearly and distinctly, but rather that I listen to the voices and appeals comprising that

[3] Page 248.

symphony of Being—which is for me, in the final analysis, a supra-rational unity beyond images, words, and concepts.[4] Nothing could be more precise. Without any allusion to the fundamental role that music has played in my life, it must be remembered that my thinking takes its departure above all from feeling, from reflection on feeling and on its implications. Moreover, all that has been said previously, and especially in Chapter III, on the impossibility of being content with a dualistic interpretation of the relations of the mind and the body, must be recalled here in its totality.

Perhaps in order to disentangle this skein of thoughts which cannot be fully apprehended except as a whole, it is best to concentrate attention here on two words that are quite simple but which encompass an infinity—*my life*—and, above all, the *fundamental situation* it presupposes. I should note in passing that my reading of Jaspers' *System of Philosophy*,[5] studied at that decisive time for me to which I am referring in this chapter, contributed greatly to my understanding of the central importance of this idea of situation which had already captured my attention a decade earlier. The peculiar quality of this fundamental situation which is mine, or which shapes me into myself, is that it can only be explored to a limited extent. Moreover, I find today that the closer I draw to my life's end the more I concern myself with those who have preceded me, with the conditions attendant upon my coming into the world—and this, when there is no longer the possibility on this side of the grave of my obtaining the clarifications which seem indispensable to me; but at the same time I am aware that at that remote period when those individuals who might have been able to enlighten me were alive, the idea of questioning them would not have entered my mind, for an invincible shyness would have restrained me. And, besides, what I would like so much to know today about them was

---

[4] Issue of December 9, 1960.
[5] *Philosophie von Karl Jaspers* (Berlin: Springer, 1932).

perhaps at that time not of a nature to be discussed or revealed; undoubtedly it was only vaguely grasped by the individuals themselves whose thought or, more exactly, whose existence, I vainly endeavor to scrutinize today.

Here there is a paradox which, it seems to me, we have not stressed sufficiently until now and which appears to me bound up with what is most tragic in our condition—that "too late," which keeps resounding in our ears when we enter the closing phase of our existence. It is only then that we feel ourselves to be, if I may venture to say so, on the same level with those who have gone before us, and we feel for them a brotherly devotion. It is only then that we can understand them—and a poignant regret consumes us at our former lack of understanding of them while they were still with us, and at our mistakes and the sorrow which they no doubt caused. It is also in this vein of thought that one of my characters—one of those with whom I most closely identified myself—expresses himself at the end of *L'Emissaire*.

"There is one thing I have discovered since my parents' death: what we call being a survivor is in reality to live not so much *after* as *under;* those we have never ceased to love with whatever is best in us become something like a living, invisible arch which we sense and even brush against, on the strength of which we are able to go on even as our powers diminish, wrenched from ourselves, toward the moment when everything will be caught up in love." [6]

Perhaps I shall have to return later to these words of Antoine Sorgue, which seem to express as nearly as possible the type of fundamental conviction around which all my thoughts as a mature man have converged. Chronologically this text is much later than those from which I am seeking to sift out the concrete meaning, since it dates from 1948. But it is related directly to the meditations on "The Mystery of the Family," [7]

[6] *Vers un autre royaume*, p. 109.
[7] *Recherche de la famille: essai sur "l'etre familial"* by G. Marcel *et al.*

developed by me during the second World War, and these
meditations, in turn, illustrate in a concrete manner the prospective affirmations of 1932 on "The Ontological Mystery." [8]
It is also from the meditations on "The Mystery of the Family," collected subsequently in *Homo Viator*, that I borrow
the long quotation which follows and which appears to me to
make comprehensible the thoughts—difficult in themselves—
around which this entire chapter gravitates:

I have to realize that behind the lighted but much restricted zone
which I call my family there stretch, to infinitude, ramifications which
at least in theory I can follow out tirelessly; only in theory, however,
for in fact an impenetrable darkness envelops this "upstream region"
of myself and prevents me from exploring any further. I can discern
enough, however, to enable me to follow this umbilical cord of my
temporal antecedents, and to see it taking shape before me, yet stretch-
ing back beyond my life in an indefinite network which, if traced
to its limits, would perhaps be coextensive with the human race itself.
My family, or rather my lineage, is the succession of historical processes by which the human species has become individualized in the
singular being that I am. All that it is possible for me to recognize
in this growing and impressive indetermination is that all these unknown human beings who stretch between me and my unimaginable
origins, whatever they may be, are not simply the causes of which
I am the effect or the product: there is no doubt that the terms "cause"
and "effect" have no meaning here. Between my ancestors and myself
a far more obscure and intimate relationship exists. I share with them
as they do with me—invisibly; they are consubstantial with me and
I with them.

By this inextricable combination of things from the past and things
to come, the mystery of the family is defined—a mystery in which I
am involved from the mere fact that I exist. Here, at the articulation
of a structure of which I can only distinguish the first traces, of a feeling which modulates between the intimate and the metaphysical—and
of an oath to be taken or refused binding me to make my own the
vague desire around which the magical fomentation of my personal
existence is centered. Such is the situation in which I find myself, I,
a creature precipitated into the tumult; thus am I introduced into this
impenetrable world.[9]

[8] See *Philosophy of Existence*.
[9] *Homo Viator*, trans. E. Craufurd (London: Gollancz, 1951), p. 71.

But undoubtedly the question will be raised: have I not been stressing the impenetrable obscurity of everything that antedates and encompasses our present being-in-the-world? And yet have I not said that mystery lies on the side of light? Is there not a contradiction here? Perhaps it would be well at this time to dispel a serious ambiguity: It is true that the light to which I refer has nothing whatever to do with the clarity which characterizes certain simple ideas as conceived, for example, by Descartes. Rather it is a question here of an illuminating source which, just because it is illuminating, is incapable of becoming an idea, or, more exactly, ideate. I use the word *source* in the sense that we speak of a source of inspiration. But all of this is really unintelligible if we do not interpose the fundamental act which, in the "Meditation" of 1933, I designated by the word "recollection," taken in its primary meaning of silent reflection or concentration of thought. I noted then that recollection, which seemed to me to have received too little attention from philosophers, is the act by which I recover my being as a unified whole, with this recovery or *reprise* assuming the aspect of a relaxation or a release. "In the depths of recollection," I wrote, "I take a stand with respect to my own life and in some way I withdraw from that life, but not at all as a pure epistemological subject. For in this withdrawal I bear with me what I am and what my life perhaps is not . . . Recollection is probably what is least spectacular in the soul. It does not consist in looking at anything; it is a *reprise*, an inner reflection, and, I would add, we may wonder if it is not the principle of unity, irrepresentable in itself, on which the very possibility of memory depends." [10]

Returning to what I said earlier concerning the source of illumination, I would add that it consists in somehow immersing one's self again in this original source beyond all utterance, and hence all conceptualization. Yet it is obvious that this act

[10] *Philosophy of Existence,* p. 12.

cannot provide the occasion for problematizing; rather it corresponds to an advance of the spirit in an exactly inverse way, precisely to the extent that it is a relaxation and a release. I would still say that only if we always bear in mind that these two approaches are the opposite of one another can we truly give meaning to the distinction between problem and mystery. It is necessary to add that recollection, and all that proceeds from it, is *meta-technical* and implies a kind of stripping away which is diametrically opposite to all savoir-faire.

It is in fact the act by which we abandon, as it were, all the powers that we possess; and as if such giving up gave rise to a certain response, yet one which is not susceptible of being anticipated in the sense that we can anticipate the outcome of an experiment. Here we should be aware of two kinds of anticipation, very different from one another. One is governed by the existence of objective relations among phenomena, whereas the other arises rather from the trust we place in a being or in reality insofar as it can be assimilated to a being. What interposes itself in the second case is rightfully called freedom.

Malebranche has already stated that freedom is a mystery, and I feel I can revive this formula for my purposes in a sense which is certainly not identical with that given the word freedom by our seventeenth-century metaphysician. What we must acknowledge is that it is useless to wish to place freedom in any way among the phenomena that come within the purview of science, and, for example, to endeavor to establish freedom on the relatively indeterminate level discussed by certain contemporary physicists. The only approach to freedom is through the reflection of a subject on himself. Properly speaking, this reflection allows me to discover—not that I am free, or that freedom is an attribute with which I could be invested—but rather that I *must* become free—that is, that my freedom must be won. Moreover, we must not fail to note the intimate relationship between the two formulas that I have successively enunciated: I am not, I have to become; I am not free, I have to become free.

Here we must try to bring together certain points which until now have been presented in somewhat random order. We must say, because of the irrefutable experience shared by all spiritual beings, that recollection as a re-establishment of contact with the source emits an illumination; this illumination can in no way be confused with the secondary kind of clarity which proceeds from what we have called the understanding. It follows on the other hand from all that has been said previously, that it would certainly be unwise to identify with Being the source itself or the light that it radiates. But in return, what seems to conform to the data of this experience (which is not technological) is the recognition that recollection bestows upon us certain resources for the exploration within ourselves that we have to make in the direction of what I have called plenitude, or the full life. If this is so, it is undoubtedly because recollection shields or protects us from all kinds of distractions that tend to estrange us from our true selves and to divert us from the unity which is at once both behind and before us.

All this, however, constitutes a scheme that is far too simple to describe the reality that I am endeavoring to explore here. There is at the outset a question which inevitably comes to mind. What relation does what I have called the "source" maintain with this upstream region of myself, the inexplorable character of which I underscored in *Homo Viator?* The response to this question, to which, I fear I have not given sufficient explanation in the past, is very difficult to formulate. Certainly we must admit that it would be possible theoretically to work out our genealogical tree, and that only contingent obstacles prevent us from doing it. But surely we must see that even if we were able to proceed with this fixing of guide marks, such an operation would be devoid of all significance. Here an observation made earlier in this chapter that may have appeared as a simple digression takes on its full meaning. But even when I limit myself to evoking those of my ancestors whom I have known or of whom I have heard, the tie that links me to them seems difficult to discern. On the one hand, they have not known me as I am or as I have to be. And on the other hand, by virtue of a sort of inexorable fatality, I myself have certainly in a very large measure misunderstood or misjudged them. Having reached an advanced stage of my life, I say, in sorrow tinged with remorse, that in an existence such as ours we have remained, each of us, in an almost thorough state of "un-knowledge." But I shall say as of now, returning to this matter at a later time, that hope, without which there is no life worthy of the name, postulates that this frustration on all sides is not final and that we shall have to find ourselves again and assemble together in the *Pleroma* which is Being; and, in the line of our destiny, we have to say at the same time that the *Pleroma* does not yet exist and that it belongs to all eternity. But I dare say that this return to the source, this recollection, is in a way a very humble anticipation of that Advent which cannot be imagined and toward which we grope our way in an all but complete obscurity.

If I have been able to speak of a spiritual itinerary, it is because we have to make our way in the world as it is, and this progress is unthinkable without a mass of data which are gradually objectified, giving rise to the innumerable problems we have to solve. It is on practical problems, in the broad sense of the word, that I shall lay principal stress in my later chapters. But what emerges from all that I have tried to show so far is that we are in danger of losing ourselves amidst these data of experience and amidst these problems unless we reestablish contact by an inverse movement with what might be called that milieu that sustains us, again without our having the right, as long as we proceed as philosophers, of substituting for this very general expression the more precise concepts used by theologians.

These difficult reflections which we all have to shape for ourselves, starting from what we are and what it is ours to live —these reflections, it is true, I have never dreamed of embodying as such in my dramatic works. On the other hand, there is no doubt that in some manner these works are imbued with them. This is especially perceptible in *Le Monde Cassé*, and it was not without reason that this play was published in 1933 with the "Meditation" to which I have so often referred.

What I am in a position to say regarding the origin of this play amounts to very little and does not relate to its deepest significance. I knew a fascinating, much admired young woman, married to a man who was not undistinguished, but quiet and dull, and to whom it seemed no one paid attention. It was on the problem of this man that I first directed my thoughts. What could he be experiencing in seeing his wife flattered and admired by men who ignored him completely? Could we not suppose that this man suffered much more from his wounded self-esteem and pride than from his love? It was possible that the young woman, discovering the kind of hidden wound her husband suffered, endeavored to help him, to bring to him a sort of balm, by making him believe that she herself was humiliated by a man who did not respond to the love which she had for him. She was thus induced by charity, by a false charity, to invent this fable of a rejected love. She notices with a kind of horror that, in effect, from the moment he believes her humiliated, her husband is drawn closer to her and shows her a sort of compassionate tenderness which only inspires her with disgust. As a consequence, she has an aversion for him, and for the first time becomes unfaithful, yielding eventually to the entreaties of a young man whom she had never taken seriously until then.

All this, however, belongs to a world which seems to have lost its inner unity, its living center—a broken world where each person is concerned only with himself. Yet, this world is not the only world. If the heroine, Christiane, has married Laurent, who loved her but whom she did not love, it was the result of a cruel disappointment. She herself, in fact, had fallen in love with a childhood friend, Jacques, and at the moment when she was going to declare her love to him, he had informed her that he was going to take monastic vows. This news chilled her. Life lost all significance for her, and hoping for nothing more, she thought that she might just as well give a little happiness to Laurent, who loved her, by consenting to marry him. But the events which unfolded subsequently now seem to her to demonstrate that in getting married under these conditions she had committed a sinful mistake. She is now distressed, and begins to wonder if she is going to leave her husband and live with this young lover whom she cannot take seriously. It is at this moment that the other world, the unbroken world, is recalled to her; and with this new stroke her confusion is increased. She has learned that Jacques, with whom it seemed to her that she would have known true happiness, has died in his monastery.

It is at this point that the monk's sister, whom Christiane had known formerly and for whom she felt no particular affection, comes to reveal to her that she had recovered the intimate notes that the monk wrote in his cell. As a consequence of a dream, he seemed to have understood too late the love that Christiane had felt for him and at the same time the harm he had done her in choosing the monastic life. From then on he felt tragically responsible for her and prayed that she would not succumb to the temptation of committing suicide, as a friend of hers, a woman of "the broken world," had recently done. Christiane is overwhelmed by this revelation. She starts by rebelling; but little by little it is as if a light enters her soul: thus in the invisible world a communion exists that she had never suspected. And immediately, as she makes the discovery that in a mysterious way she participates in this

other world which had been Jacques', she comes to take a
stand regarding her life and to condemn it. But at the same
time she cannot continue to go on living the lie in which she
has imprisoned herself through her infidelity. She feels she
must reveal the truth to her husband and by that means renew or tighten the sacred bond which was on the point of
breaking. Laurent staggers under the weight of this revelation.
He even starts by revolting and then he is won over by the
spirit of truth which has taken hold of Christiane; and at least
during a brief moment—as had happened to Roger and Clare
at the end of *Le Quatuor*—these two human beings feel as one.
With this instantaneous realization the work ends, and certainly nothing guarantees that this accord will last. But at least
they will, at the apex of their life, have achieved true unity:
they will have freed themselves from the broken world.

This entire ending has been challenged and disputed. Certain critics have spoken of a *deus ex machina* and of something contrived. I feel, however, that in principle I had the
right to end the play in this way, because experience has
shown irrefutably, and no doubt much more often than is
commonly believed—that following an encounter, a light may
arise in a soul and at the same time that soul may in turn become illuminating. In fact, I met a Hungarian of the Benedic-
tine Order who, apropos of this play, told me that he had
known a strikingly similar case.

Naturally, one can object that what counts is plausibility;
and it is in fact true that in the perspective of *Le Monde cassé*
this plausibility is lacking. But in response to this objection
we must reply, it seems to me, that in the world as it is actually
given to us, this break—to which I shall refer again—is not
radical, and the very fact of interrogating one's self concerning Being, of putting one's self in the presence of the mystery
of Being, is sufficient to show it. The unforgivable mistake
would be to introduce a contrivance—to utilize in some way
what we may call the supernatural—as a device for resolving

the tragic problems posed for man today. But I will have to show in later chapters that the denouement of *Le Monde cassé* constitutes an exception among my works and that very often the final stress is put rather on the interrogative note. This latter is, moreover, tied to an ambiguity the principle of which resides in the very structure of our being. But there is the further danger in this domain of making oneself a prisoner of a formula. My persistent effort has, perhaps more than anything else, consisted in struggling against the temptation of any formula whatsoever, and this in the name of human experience which we must confront in all its complexity, aware of the incessant interplay of light and shadow suffusing the whole of our existence.

VI ◂

The Self and Ambiguity

Having traveled thus far, we should, it seems to me, ask ourselves how near we have come to the goal I set for myself at the beginning. In stressing, as I have done, the mystery of Being and the positive value of recollection, we may ask whether or not we are in a position to see more clearly the essential nature of what we call human dignity. At first glance, it seems we can at least make a first discovery: a person capable of communing with himself and so of renewing contact with an invisible and limitless reality thereby reveals himself capable of transcending the spontaneous course of life. But here, are we not simply following Pascal when he says: "All the dignity of man consists in thought. Thought is therefore by its nature a wonderful and incomparable thing." He adds immediately, however: "It must have strange defects to be contemptible. In fact, its magnitude is such that nothing is more ridiculous. How great it is in its nature! How vile it is in its defects!" [1] This disparaging remark, indicating what thought can and does become, considerably limits the significance of Pascal's first proposition. Today, especially, in the light of the development of modern psychology, we are inclined, generally speaking, not so much to overrate thought as an invaluable privilege, as to emphasize the fact that it exists,

[1] *Pensées*, ed. Leon Brunschvig, 3 vols., 1904, p. 496.

first of all, as a function to insure the adaptation of an individual to his natural and social milieus—in short, to reduce it to a system of delicate mechanisms which, at times, may fail to work properly, and thus may defeat their purpose. Under these circumstances, if we speak here of transcendence, it is in the very limited sense, and one may doubt that in such a perspective it is possible to repeat that all the dignity of man consists in thought.

On the other hand, what we have said of recollection shows distinctly that this can in no way be reduced to thought as mechanism. We have seen that it is a *source* of thought rather than thought itself. It implies the freedom with which I disengage myself and withdraw from my own life in order to be able to evaluate it and even eventually to censure it. But, at the same time, it becomes possible for me to start off again in another direction, guided by this light which has been bestowed upon me I do not know *by whom*. Indeed, I am not even sure that the question *"by whom?"* may have a precise meaning here. It seems rather that this light shines through the world of the "who's" and "what's" in the midst of which I am accustomed to move and to which I constantly refer when, for example, I ask myself *to whom* a particular thing belongs, *who* said this or wrote that letter, and so on . . . Must we then speak of impersonality? I think, rather, that a subtle distinction must be made between the impersonal and the suprapersonal. A law is impersonal; we might term it "contents"; it is a "what," a "something." But the light we have spoken of, to the extent that it lights the different "contents," whatever they may be, reveals that it is not of the same nature. To put it differently, we may say that it cannot be assimilated to a concept or to anything that can be conceptualized.

We could perhaps even at this point answer the question I asked at the beginning of this chapter by saying that man's essential characteristic seems to be his ability to let himself be penetrated by this supra-personal light, an ability which is evidently linked in some way to what we call human dignity.

However, I do not think that this answer can be considered final. The answer we have here is oversimplified; it does not take into account the concrete circumstances in which life unfolds. The truth is, as I pointed out at the end of my last chapter, that we are obliged to focus our attention on the obstacles encountered by what we may call the will to commune, or, using a different language but one homologous to the preceding, on all that contributes not only to separate us from Being, but even to make the quest for Being appear illusory and, finally, meaningless. We could at this juncture refer to the notion of alienation which Marx, following Hegel, strongly emphasized, but in a particular context, and undoubtedly without realizing its full import (while Hegel, on the contrary, was fully aware of it).

Only a close scrutiny of alienation can enable us to resist the temptation of the philosophy of idealism to which so many have yielded who are prone to substitute for the study of man as he actually is elaborations on what he *should be*, or on the too-flattering self-portrait he is likely to draw when his attention is focused on an essence imprudently dissociated from the existential context.

As I say this, I wish to point out that I am far from endorsing existentialism as defined by Sartre; besides, this extreme existentialism I have never accepted. All I wish to do is to assert the rights of a phenomenology in the light of which the primacy of experience over what could be called pure thought must be rigorously preserved.

Surely it is not a coincidence that less than a year after attempting to define what I called the "approaches" to the ontological mystery I felt the need of concentrating my thought on *having*. It was, however, ten years earlier, in the *Metaphysical Journal* of March 16, 1923, that I mentioned for the first time how important it was to make a distinction between what one *has* and what one *is*. "Only," I wrote, "it is exceedingly difficult to give it the form of a concept, and yet this should be possible." And I continued:

What one *has* is seemingly, to a certain extent, exterior to oneself. And yet this exteriority is not absolute. In principle, one *has* things, or what can be assimilated to things, and in the precise measure in which this assimilation is possible. I can *have*, strictly speaking, only some thing whose existence is to a certain extent independent of myself. In other words, what I have can be added to myself. Moreover, the fact of its being possessed by me can be added to other properties, other qualities, and so on . . . belonging to the thing I have. I have only what I can, in some way and within certain limits, make use of, in other words insofar as I can be considered a power, a being endowed with powers.[2]

This introductory text was to be placed at the beginning of a "brief study of a phenomenology of the having." But I was also to be influenced, though to what degree I would not be able to say today, by at least a partial reading of the work of the German philosopher Gunther Stern, known today by the name of Gunther Anders. The book, entitled *Über das Haben*, was published in Bonn in 1928.[3]

It is a fact, however, that all my thoughts on *having* originated from those I had previously pursued on Incarnation. It seemed to me that here the fundamental fact was what could be called "attachment" to the body proper. In this connection we may consider the French phrase: "tenir à ce qu'on possède" (to be attached to one's possessions). If someone snatches an object from us to which we are attached because it belongs to us, we feel as if we were physically injured. But, at the same time, this shows how dependent we are on what we possess. I wrote somewhere: "Nos possessions nous dévorent" ("We are devoured by our possessions"). This truth, if I am not mis-

---

[2] *Metaphysical Journal*, p. 311.
[3] Gunther Stern, *Über das Haben: sieben Kapitel zur Ontologie der Erkenntnis* (Bonn: F. Cohen, 1928).

taken, has been very forcefully expressed by Henry James in
The Spoils of Poynton.

In my *Phénoménologie de l'Avoir,* I stressed certain aspects
of the subject which are still important to me today: first, what
I called a repressed dynamism. I would perhaps express myself somewhat differently now. To say I possess this particular
object is to imply that I can make use of it, lend it, give it, or,
as the case may be, destroy it, without anyone having—I do
not stay the physical power, but the *right* to stop me. However, the word "repressed" no longer seems to me adequate.
The truth is that I hold in reserve, as it were, these possible
actions which perhaps I shall not perform. The *having* falls
here under the category of property, but it is obvious that it
is more comprehensive than property, and it may be in this
particular respect that the philosopher is more directly concerned. Here again, reference to the body is extremely instructive. If I say I have a nose or eyes, it is apparent at once
that the word "possession" very inadequately expresses what
I mean. Yet, as I have indicated, it seems that to this *having,*
which is perhaps impossible to define, every sort of possession may be related. Here is a paradox which cannot be too
strongly emphasized: something possessed is related in some
manner to a *having* that cannot itself be defined in terms of
possession. It is, moreover, exactly in this way that any instrument appears as the extension of a power which is not itself
instrumental in the strictest sense of the word.

Nevertheless, it may not be amiss to point out that, in a certain context, the subject can be tempted to treat his body as
an object he can use freely. To understand this, one can take
as an example the emancipated girl who tells her parents that
her body belongs to her, that she can do what she pleases with
it. But in this case we should not overlook the fact that it is
actually for herself that she wants her freedom, her body being
for her a kind of materialized equivalent of herself. Experience
may show her—and in many ways—that this freedom has

limits she did not suspect, that the body can be only imperfectly controlled, if, for example, she finds herself pregnant.

These remarks are intended to serve as a background for what follows. I wish now to try to clarify my meaning when I state that I have an idea or that I have a feeling. It seems at first that there is nothing here but darkness and confusion, or, to put it more exactly, that we are confronted with a very wide keyboard. At one end of this keyboard we find the impression or the idea which takes possession of us at a given moment, but which will be replaced by another idea or another impression, this change being effected at the surface of ourselves, and, it would seem, without anything like an implantation taking place. It is evident that in this extreme case the word "having" becomes void of any precise meaning.

At the other end of this keyboard, we shall find, for example, the fact of having a conviction (moral, religious, or political). This conviction may appear to me as being consubstantial with myself, as being part of myself. But then, should we not ask ourselves if *having* does not tend to pass into *being*. The answer is not simple, and I am not sure that in the past I have made myself sufficiently clear on this point. I commented some time ago that *having* is something which can be exposed, a remark which can be applied either to the conviction or to the object possessed. But I can expose only that which, in a certain manner, is or can become exterior to me. It may happen, moreover, that an idea I considered mine, once it is exposed, becomes detached from me, as it were. It could also be said figuratively that it becomes devitalized, or loses its bloom and withers. Thus I find that this idea did not have as firm, as intimate, a hold on me as I had thought before I tried to propose it to others. It proved that in some way it can be detached, that it can fall from me as a leaf falls from a tree.

This leads us to a recognition of the vast difference between the exposable idea or conviction, and belief in the truest sense, which can only be attested, that is, can hardly be anything but someone's testimony. Here *having* seems really to pass into *being*. But this is true only in its extreme form, in the person who lives and radiates his belief, that is to say, above all, in the saint. However, it is no less evident that in the ordinary and imperfect believer this faith of which, if he is sincere, he wishes to be the living incarnation, is covered, as it were, by an overgrowth of accepted opinions, prejudices, habits, which he may be said to possess. And if I have said that no one of us knows exactly and cannot know what he believes, it is precisely that what is given to his "knowing consciousness," if I may use this term, is precisely that combination of elements which can be exposed or shown, but nevertheless remains truly exterior to him, as I have said. His faith he will know only by the manner in which he will be brought to acknowledge that he does attest it. Yet the truth is still a great deal more complex. Actually it may happen that in some particular cases he discovers that, through weakness or cowardice, he is *incapable* of attesting it. But if this discovery of his inadequacy affects him deeply and painfully, it proves to him, none the less, the reality of his belief, although his testimony remains inarticulate, as it were, and cannot be conveyed to others.

It is quite clear, however, that when it comes to attesting one's faith, this inadequacy or imperfection is generally found in those who consider themselves, or are considered, believers, the word "believer" not necessarily being taken in a purely religious sense. Here again I shall quote the words of a character in *L'Emissaire*, Antoine Sorgue, who, though not my mouthpiece, is one of those who show the greatest awareness of the fundamental situation which is our concern.

Antoine. Yes and no, Sylvie, this is the only answer when we ourselves are concerned: we believe and we do not believe, we love and we do not love, we are and we are not. But if this is so, it is because we are heading toward a goal which at the same time we see and we do not see.[4]

4 *Vers un autre royaume*, p. 108.

These words, which could serve as an epigraph to these lectures, and to all my work for that matter, take their full meaning in the light of these reflections on having, and still more precisely from the fact that having, to the extent that it depends upon Incarnation, cannot in any way be set up as an absolute or be considered sufficient in itself.

Yet it is necessary to carry our analysis one step further and, as we may already have surmised on our way, to come to the consideration of the self and of the essential ambiguity which detracts from its purity, so to speak. The transition can be made easily here by referring to my previous remarks on the attachment to oneself which is implied in any affirmation of having as such.

Modern idealism, particularly in Fichte and the Romanticists, has, it is true, seen in the self the thetic, and consequently the creative, principle *par excellence*. But for that it was necessary, I might say, to "transcendentalize" the self, that is, to substitute for the empirical self a unifying, universal principle. And then only by dialectical feats can one attempt to extract the empirical self from the absolute or merely transcendental self. In the same way one will have to stress, above all, the limitations inherent in the empirical self considered as such. Thus will be brought to light the opposition between the two principles which cannot be designated by the same word, *moi* (self), without creating the most dangerous confusion. This is sufficient to explain the fact that after the Romanticists—and notably in Hegel—the idea of the absolute *moi* was practically discarded.

As far as I am concerned, my life experience and the reflections to which it led me, have made me emphasize more and more that the *moi* serves much more as a shutter (as in a camera) than as a true creative principle. At the most elementary level, I shall refer to the English word "self-conscious," in its pejorative connotation which the French *conscient de soi*, does not have, any more than the German *selbstbewusst*. The English word indicates as strongly as possible the fact that the self, when it is, as it were, encumbered with itself, stands as a screen between one's consciousness and others. More precisely, the subject is as though paralyzed by the often quite false picture he imagines others have of him. It is hardly necessary to indicate that this is one of the roots of timidity. If we follow this observation, we see clearly how indispensable it is to distinguish between "I" which, it may be noted, cannot be treated as a substantive, and "myself" or "the self" which supposes a certain reflection, taken in a kind of optic sense. We must also notice that the current use of the Latin word "ego" in English philosophical language has the serious disadvantage of omitting or of precluding this important distinction. As I wrote in *Homo Viator*,[5] we shall have to see in what I call *moi* (myself) an emphasis which I give, not to my entire experience, but to that portion or aspect of my experience I mean particularly to protect from a certain attack or infraction which may jeopardize it. In this sense, it has often been pointed out, and rightly so, that it is impossible to assign precise limits to this *moi*. I added that this *moi* cannot be separated from *here, now*, and I said I could not see how a being for whom there would be neither *here* nor *now* could still appear to himself as *moi*. I added that under these conditions the emphasis I mentioned before should tend to hold itself as an enclave, but a moving and vulnerable enclave: an enclosure which is alive; and, to justify this term, I referred to the so far unsurpassed portrait of the egoist in Meredith's novel of that title. Today, however, I wonder if, in the text I just referred to, I should not have dwelt more than I did on the obturating capacity of this enclave. The egotist, or, in the most precise sense of the word, the egoist, like Willoughby, is rendered incapable of seeing what precisely his *moi* hides from him. Another person counts for him only in relation to this *moi*, insofar as he appreciates it, respects it, admires it, and so on . . . We may recall the part

[5] See pp. 13–28.

played in the novel by Laetitia Dale. Willoughby needs her to the extent that she brings to him the constant confirmation of, shall we say, his own judgment of himself. This may be too intellectual a way of describing a relation to oneself which is more akin to self-enjoyment. Yet it may be necessary to add that along with this self-enjoyment there is very often a gnawing anxiety which, of course, one refuses to acknowledge, although it remains present as a secret threat to be warded off at any cost.

Here we find again our previous reflections on having—at least where having is, properly speaking, possession. I would note in passing that in French and also, it seems, in English, this word can be both active and passive, and this seems to me very revealing. In a sense it is true to say that to possess is to be possessed, precisely because possession is not free from a secret anxiety the nature of which is not fundamentally different, it seems, from the anxiety we find in the egoist as portrayed in the fullest sense by Meredith. Besides, it is evident that egoism (selfishness) takes innumerable forms, and it is only when carried to the extreme that it becomes, properly speaking, egotism.

All these observations will appear of the greatest importance to anyone who tries to probe the intersubjective relations and go to their very root. Here we are at the very center of the area I have tried to explore as a dramatist, although at the outset I did not make any attempt to state precisely the general philosophical meaning of the concrete cases which fell under my mental gaze.

Following the method I used in my earlier chapters, I propose to examine those of my plays which seem to me today the most significant in the light of the foregoing observations. The case I treated in *La Chapelle ardente* is, if not the simplest, at any rate the clearest, the least subject to controversy, but not the least painful. I shall describe it here from the point of view of the central character; it goes without saying that other descriptions are possible when the other three characters are considered.

The action takes place at the end of the first World War in a country house where Aline Fortier lives with her husband, Colonel Octave Fortier, a career officer who resigned his commission after the signing of the peace treaty. Their only son, Raymond, was killed at the front, and Aline thinks her husband is to a certain degree responsible for his death. In the first place, he more or less urged him to enlist. Furthermore, he took him into his own regiment for officer's training and did not object to his being sent on the dangerous mission in which he met his death. Aline's feelings for her husband are therefore a mixture of resentment and horror. Besides, she says, he enjoyed war, which she herself considers inexcusable butchery. The Fortiers have taken into their home Mireille Pradole, Raymond's fiancée, who is an orphan. It is around the girl's destiny that the play revolves. Aline regards her as a reminder of her son whom she idolized and now fairly worships. She could not bear the idea of Mireille's loving another man. For her this would be worse than a betrayal, an intolerable lesion. We find here what I said previously about the "enclave"—vulnerable, like an open wound. Raymond, the son she worships and whose loss leaves her all the more disconsolate since she has no religious beliefs and cannot imagine any after-life for him except in herself, is, I might say, the most essential part of her *moi*, though she is unable to realize it. She is not aware of the fact that for the real individual that was Raymond she substituted a kind of idol which is one with herself. By no means should Mireille of her own free will destroy this idol into which she has been incorporated by Aline.

Now it so happens that on a neighboring estate lives a handsome young man just out of the army. He meets Mireille on the tennis court and is visibly attracted by her. For Aline he immediately represents a threat to be warded off. But of course nothing would be gained if Mireille had to give him up and make a sacrifice. She must be persuaded that she is not in love with him. And to this end Aline's actions will be directed. Subtly she will try to convince Mireille that, being the girl she is, and, moreover, the one who was going to share the life of a man such as Raymond, she cannot seriously consider marrying this playboy. Here Aline takes advantage of the fact that Mireille admires her and would not, for anything in the world, disappoint one she calls "mother." Yet, at the same time, something in Mireille's soul desperately struggles against this powerful influence on her of a person made tyrannical because she is possessed by one idea, one love.

Aline realizes, however, that in spite of everything Mireille will have to make a new start in life. Still, it must be with a man who cannot in any way compare with Raymond as he was in real life, a man who, in short, will not overshadow or destroy the idol. Now it happens that Colonel Fortier has a nephew, André, a sickly boy who suffers from a heart ailment and for that reason was declared unfit for military service. He feels inferior, and considers himself worthless. He loves Mireille, but without hope, and he has never dared confess his love to her. Aline learns that, unknown to him, his condition has been found hopeless by the cardiologist he has just come to consult once more. From now on, an idea takes shape in her, that of suggesting to Mireille a marriage which would be an act of charity, of pure sacrifice, and which would not give offense to Raymond's image. Still she must proceed in such a way that Mireille, who has her pride, will think that this is a free act, an act which she can regard as absolutely true to the best in herself. She must not think that she acted to please Aline. In other words, the question for Aline will be to influence, by clever maneuvering, another's freedom, but in such a way as to make this freedom appear to have been entirely preserved.

But reality is still more complex: for Aline cannot let herself

be made aware of exercising an influence. She must be made
to imagine that Mireille herself contemplates this marriage out
of pity after she has turned away from the other man, the one
Aline does not want. Thus dishonesty is the mainspring of the
action, but, as frequently or always happens, it is not conscious of itself; it can regard itself as sincerity. Incidentally,
I may say that *La Chapelle ardente* anticipates the analyses
of bad faith and self-deception which Sartre was to develop
with remarkable success twenty years later in *Being and Nothingness.*[6]

I shall leave aside here the ending of the play, an ending
which is, in fact, no conclusion. For to me there could be no
question of ending it with a breaking off, a death or a suicide.
As in almost all of my plays, the denouement consists in the
resolution of a certain significant accord which may be a dis-
sonance. Here André and Mireille are married. They experience a weak kind of intimacy which may appear, at least to
André, as happiness. But Aline is always present and manages
to do evil when she wants to do good, but good according to
her own standards. Mireille, who in retrospect sees clearly,
says some very harsh words to her and Aline goes away. But
if she is driven to desperation, won't she be tempted to take
her own life? This would be dreadful and must be avoided
at all costs. They call her back, knowing that they will never
be able to get rid of her. "Do you really think she is a wicked
woman?" André asks Mireille. And she answers: "No, she is
a woman to be pitied."

In this play, as in most of the others, I have sought to introduce a maximum of lucidity and at the same time a maximum
of compassion. I think as Mireille does when she regains her
composure: Aline is not a wicked woman, she has no ill will,
but all her acts are governed by the kind of possession I men-

⁶ Jean-Paul Sartre, *Being and Nothingness: An Essay on Phenomenological Ontology.* Translated and with introduction by H. E. Barnes (New
York: Philosophical Library, 1956).

tioned before. And I should add that, in her, suffering, far
from having a purifying influence, has literally intoxicated
her. There is not, I think, a more unsound idea than that often
developed by authors of edifying treatises—the idea that suffering may be regarded as good in itself. I should be more
inclined to say that, on the contrary, it is bad in principle,
although the human soul, under certain favorable conditions,
when it has created around itself the appropriate spiritual climate, can freely—I mean by a free act—transmute this suffering not exactly into something good, but into a principle
capable of radiating love, hope, and charity. Yet it is necessary that the suffering soul, through suffering itself, should
open itself up more to others, instead of closing in upon itself
and its wound. This is precisely what a person like Aline cannot do. Can we blame her? Must we say, on the contrary, that
grace was denied her? But, as I shall have occasion to repeat
later on, it does not seem possible to think of grace without
reference to a certain breadth and inner readiness. It may be,
therefore, that Aline is in some way responsible for this lack
or this dispossession. But who among us could say for sure?
We have to understand and pity her rather than judge her.

This play, written shortly after the end of the first World
War and without reference to any philosophical idea, I have
analyzed at length to show that it deals with the most fundamental problems. These cannot be solved by the dramatist,
however. The very idea of a solution in this perspective seems
absurd. The question is rather to hold up to the spectator a
sort of magic mirror in which he finds his own problems, his
own difficulties, with the result that through the mediation
of the drama itself there will emerge this awareness which,
most of the time, remains in us as though benumbed and inarticulate.

This applies to all my dramatic works, in particular to
such plays as *Un Homme de Dieu* and *Le Chemin de crête*
(*Ariadne* in the English version). But in these two works,

ambiguity will be much more clearly perceptible than in *La Chappelle ardente*, though here, too, its presence is almost constantly felt in the discrepancy between what the characters really are and the idea of themselves which they or their own interests present to them.

The main character of *Un Homme de Dieu* is a Protestant minister, Claude Lemoine. Twenty years earlier, when he lived in a village in the Ardèche, his wife Edmée confessed to him that she had been unfaithful to him. Her lover, a certain Michel Sandier, is actually the father of Osmonde, whom Claude believed to be his legitimate child. Claude forgave his wife, and life followed its normal, monotonous course, first in an industrial town of northern France, later in Paris. An unexpected turn of events is going to change the situation: The former lover, Michel Sandier, whom the Lemoines had lost sight of, suffers from an incurable disease, and, through his physician, Claude's brother, asks to see his daughter once more before he dies. Edmée's immediate and spontaneous reaction is that they must refuse. (Osmonde, of course, does not know the truth.) Claude, on the contrary, feels there would be a certain cowardice in opposing a request which is, after all, legitimate. Wouldn't such refusal show that the past is not entirely forgotten? But Edmée, as woman, is hurt by this scruple or by this magnanimous attitude. It seems to her that Claude does not act as a man would act, but as someone to whom charity is a profession. And, she asks herself, has he ever been a real man? Thus, once again, the question is raised of the value of this forgiveness which, it now seems to her, Claude had managed to make so oppressive to her. She recalls that before her confession of infidelity Claude had had religious doubts which had seemed afterward to disappear. If his love had been of a sensual kind, could he have shown himself so noble? Perhaps his forgiving her had been only a professional act, void of substance, which at the same time gave him the comfortable feeling that he had chosen the right calling.

Thus, the whole past is made to unfold again, as it were, by the situation Claude and Edmée have to face today. Nor is this all. In the course of the scene in which she is again face to face with her former lover, Edmée herself will be led to ask herself for what reasons she was compelled to confess her guilt to her husband. With extraordinary lucidity, Michel, who seems to have passed from this life already, forces her to ask herself if she did not act out of sheer cowardice, for he had asked her to go away with him. Was it not true that she was afraid of all the risks involved and that she had escaped through confession because she knew that Claude, being the man he was, would forgive her, and that with his forgiveness she could find again the kind of moral comfort so necessary to her?

Thus, by raising the question of their own motives and of the meaning of their acts in the past, Claude and Edmée come to destroy each other, and this destruction will not be without consequences for others. Their daughter, Osmonde, is in love with a much older man, who lives in the same house and whose children she sometimes takes care of, since his wife is in an insane asylum. Claude will eventually tell her the truth about her birth, but under circumstances which will lead the girl to question, in her turn, the value of his acts. Reacting against this impure combination of virtues, or mock-virtues, and cowardice, Osmonde will decide to serve as governess for the children of the man who loves her but who has scruples regarding their relationship. In fact, she will decide to give herself to him and thus break away from all the compromises that go with conventionality.

But the essential element of the drama is the part played in it by the inquiring mind. Claude, in particular, cannot know for sure what took place in him or for him when he forgave his wife twenty years before, and perhaps Edmée's mistake lies in the fact that, yielding to a need springing from her ego, that avid and vulnerable ego I spoke of before, she questions again the value of Claude's forgiveness. And today, think-

ing again of this play I wrote forty years ago—one that had
the greatest number of performances of all my plays in France
and abroad—I can add something I certainly was not aware
of when I wrote the play: Claude's forgiving his wife was
an act which had real meaning and value only at the time it
was performed, aside from all the questions that might later
be raised about it. Furthermore, is it not only useless but even
wrong to question, twenty years after the event, the motives
of an act which is so far removed from both husband and
wife? In the final scene—the one I like best, perhaps—both
Claude and Edmée come to acknowledge that they no longer
know if they really loved each other, or what their love was
like, or what had caused it. For one brief moment Claude
is tempted to commit suicide. But no, he must not forget that
good people who in no way suspect what he is going through
and naïvely look upon him as a saint, need him, and that, in
fact, he has been and will continue to be of real service to
them. This, however, is only a sort of pragmatic consolation
with which the man of God he is—despite everything—cannot be entirely satisfied. The only recourse left to him is
prayer, the calling upon Him *who knows him as he is,* while he
himself, groping his way through life, has always misjudged
himself or seen himself as he is not.

Here again there is evidence of anticipation in relation to
everything which, later on, was to find articulate expression
at the level of pure thought. Needless to say, all this can be
clarified a posteriori by views on the ontological mystery; yet
at the same time it gives content and substance to what, considered in itself, might seem only idle speculation. It is in fact
much more than that. It is the seal of reflection on an experience of a truly unusual type, since it is lived only through
imaginary characters, but, let it be emphasized again, without
their owing anything to preconceived ideas they would afterward come to embody. If this experience proved to be rich

in philosophical developments, it is, I am sure, precisely because of this lack of preconceived ideas.

This applies specifically to *Le Chemin de crête*, undoubtedly the most important of the three plays I have undertaken to discuss here. In it, circumstances and situations play a most important role, which leads us to what seems to me a highly significant observation: While in the philosophies of the classical type—Plato's or Berkeley's, for example—the dialogue was between persons with only slightly individualized characters, it is perfectly understandable that, in an existential philosophy, the process should be reversed and that in a theater which is, so to speak, the other side of this philosophy, individualization should be stressed, not only in the characters but also in the situations in which they are involved. Lacking this, we should remain in the abstract in which existential thought can have no place.

I shall limit myself here to a summary of *Le Chemin de crête*, though the play actually is extremely complex.

Ariane Leprieur's poor health has obliged her to spend many years of her life in the mountains. But she insists that her husband Jérome should not sacrifice himself any longer and should return to Paris to resume his activities as a music critic. The relations between the two are all the more involved since Ariane is wealthy, while Jérome has no money of his own. He depends on her financially, a position he finds difficult to bear, though his wife strives to convince him that she is only too happy to make life easier for him. In Paris, Jérome has an affair with Violette Masargue, a young musician who has already been unhappy in love. Ariane learns of this affair and decides to go and spend a few months in Paris. She wants to get acquainted with Violette and asks her to give her a few piano lessons. She tells her that she knows everything, that she has no grudge either against her or against Jérome, but that Jérome must be kept ignorant of the fact that his

wife has learned of the affair; she is sure he could not bear
the thought and perhaps would be driven to a desperate decision. A strange intimacy, therefore, is going to bring the two
women together which Jérome will find surprising and irritat-
ing. What, then, is Ariane's intention? Why this forgiving
attitude and, at the same time, this desire for secrecy? Isn't
there something disturbing and impure in the impassioned
interest she takes in her husband's mistress? Jérome, exasper-
ated, declares he has made up his mind to get a divorce and
marry Violette. But the latter, who has developed a sincere
affection for Ariane, an affection not unmixed with a feeling
of remorse and anxiety, feels it would be gross treason to
steal her husband. She tells Ariane in confidence what Jérome's
intentions are and asks her what she should do. After paus-
ing to reflect a moment, Ariane seems to accept calmly—or
with resignation—the idea of a divorce. Nevertheless, what
she will tell Violette from now on seems precisely intended
to dissuade her from the project. She points out to her that
Jérome is poor; she, Violette, has no money and has a child
to bring up. Will Jérome, who likes luxury, be satisfied with
a precarious existence? Ariane ends by suggesting that Violette
permit her to help the couple financially, but without Jérome's
knowing anything about it, since his pride would not allow
him to accept such an arrangement. But all the vague sus-
picions Violette had entertained about Ariane are now suddenly confirmed, and she explodes. It becomes obvious to her
that Ariane has treacherously—and purposely—used every
means at her disposal to destroy her relationship with Jérome.
Ariane does not answer these accusations, but a little later she
simply observes that, if she comes to die, Violette should know
she forgave her this outburst. Is she sincere? Are Violette's
accusations justified? How is one to know? However, at the
end of the play, and without my going into the details, Ariane
will also come to have doubts about herself. She will see that
she cannot be entirely sure of her real motives. In other words,

she will become aware of this ambiguity which has been gradually disclosed to the spectator. However, unlike Claude Lemoine, she has no religious faith; her only recourse will be that of so many others—to write a diary which will probably be published and may be fairly successful. Yet, at the same time, she has no illusions about the value of such an escape: for literature is only one way of escaping, and, in this, this tragedy of ambiguity ends with the same appeal as *Un Homme de Dieu*—an inarticulate cry for help but with no faith to guide it.

This play is undoubtedly one of the most somber I have ever written, a fact which may have been surprising to some, since it came several years after my conversion to Catholicism. But I have never truly admitted that this conversion should entail the obligation to close each of my works with what I might call an orthodox ending. To my way of thinking, this would be nothing but deception. The fact of belonging to the Catholic Church, or to any church, does not—indeed, should not—prevent us from seeking to understand, with a lucidity which must never exclude compassion, how life appears to those who are enlightened by no belief of a transcendental nature. It is for this very reason that I have never agreed to be labeled a Catholic philosopher or a Catholic writer, for to accept a label of this kind is, I fear, to pledge oneself, in the name of misdirected proselytizing, to something false, incompatible with that intellectual honesty which has constantly appeared to me as the first duty, not only of the philosopher—which goes without saying—but also of the writer; and by this I mean in particular the novelist or the dramatist.

VII ◄

Human Dignity

I F it is possible for me to take an over-all view of the spiritual journey I have undertaken to describe in this book, I am tempted to think now that the year 1936 marked a decisive turn in my life. In May 1936, a new government was formed, known as the Popular Front. The failure of this coalition cannot be denied by anyone today. One sign of this failure was the fact that Léon Blum and his associates not only were unable to avert the threat of war already existing at that time, but undoubtedly by their illusions and their weakness contributed to making the conflict inevitable. Besides, it should not be forgotten that Léon Blum declared in 1932 that Hitler would never be able to seize power. It can be asserted now that a clear-sighted statesman, aware of the danger presented by Hitlerism, could have held the Führer back and perhaps driven him to suicide. It is true that the Rhineland had been remilitarized before Léon Blum came to power. But the same spirit of surrender was to be found in everyone, with the exception of a few Rightists whose influence was almost nil at that time; and that spirit of surrender was concealed only by an anti-Fascist rhetoric in which no clear intelligence could place any trust.

This reference to the political events of that period may be surprising in the present context. Yet it seems indispensable.

For, thus confronted by historical circumstances which I think I am in a position to say I felt immediately as exceptionally grave, my prospective thought, as always on the dramatic and not specifically philosophic level, began to experience what it is no exaggeration to describe as a change of focus. By this I mean that the anthropological problem, considered of course in its ethical aspect, became for me at that time increasingly acute.

It could not be said, however, that there was a complete break in my evolution. The dramas of ambiguity which I analyzed in the preceding chapter presuppose and at the same time give evidence of a complete reappraisal of the human being as such. It may even be said that if we compare *Le Chemin de crête* with *Un Homme de Dieu*, the evolution which I am trying to clarify here is already apparent. *Un Homme de Dieu* closed with a prayer, an anguished appeal to Him who alone knows me as I am: in other words, the theocentric reference remained explicit there. This is no longer the case in *Le Chemin de crête*. The heroine, having reached the stage of being absolutely in the dark about her own nature and her own worth, no doubt appeals to invisible powers to come to her assistance, but she has not even a name for them, and perhaps she no longer considers them distinct from the noblest parts of herself. The truth is that Ariane will never escape from the labyrinth. Liberation for her can be effected only through the medium of the written word, diary-writing, an extremely illusory liberation by which not even she herself can be deceived.

In this play, one can already hear, though still rather faintly, disturbing echoes of the events of the outside world, and it is possible to imagine that the uneasiness felt by all the characters without exception, though in no way explained by the increasing confusion on the political scene, is, however, an expression of this confusion and, as it were, a microcosmic projection of it.

But *Le Dard*, written a few months later, during the first weeks of 1936, and therefore slightly before the events which I have just recalled, includes a specific reference both to the Hitler threat, which had been constantly growing in the three previous years, and to the evolution which was becoming more apparent among Leftist intellectuals, the very ones who were to champion the Popular Front. But need I say that this evolution was not to stop after the terrible hiatus of the war and the Occupation? *Le Dard* develops the theme to which, fifteen years later, I was to give articulate expression on the philosophical level in the introduction to *Les Hommes contre l'humain* [1] entitled "L'Universel contre les masses." I wish to point out here that my original intention was to give this title to the whole book. I yielded, however, to the wishes of my publisher, who, of course, thought it lacked commercial appeal. Today, however, I feel that the title under which the book appeared, *Les Hommes contre l'humain*, is much less faithful to my essential purpose.

And so we come, at the end of the singularly tortuous path we have followed, to the central problems I had stated at the beginning of this book and which, under various forms, will, almost without interruption, be our primary consideration to the very end. It is actually on the essence of human dignity that the conflict in *Le Dard* is focused, and this conflict is between Professor Eustache Soreau and the German singer, Werner Schnee.

As is almost always the case, I find it difficult to be very precise about the origin of this work. The few preparatory notes I was able to lay my hands on do not enable me to find out from where, as we say in French, "l'idée est sortie." It should be pointed out that the word "sortir," when applied to a thought, has always a somewhat vague meaning and corresponds to a metaphor which cannot be made explicit: that of a light suddenly issuing from darkness. All I can say with

[1] See *Man against Humanity* in Author's Works Cited.

certainty is that in a certain essayist of the Left, who came
from a family of very modest means, I thought I had sensed
or, at any rate, imagined, the bad conscience which is the
distinctive characteristic of my hero. A book recently published by this writer makes me think that in reality he re-
sembled my Eustache Soreau much less than I thought, for
it reveals that, unlike the hero of my play, he had a Christian
upbringing.

It is of course necessary to keep in mind here my central
observation: otherwise, the references to my dramatic works,
as I have said repeatedly, lose all their significance. No more
here than elsewhere did I start from abstract ideas to be
dramatically illustrated afterwards. In other words, I did not
have in mind two different or even opposite conceptions of
man and of his essential dignity. On the contrary, this opposition took shape in relation to the two central characters and
to the concrete situation in which they are involved. It should
be further understood that the spectator (or the reader) is
urged to go beyond the particular case presented to him in
order to find its essential significance. We may add that this
significance is in the strongest sense of the word an historical
one; that is to say, it cannot be fully perceived without reference to the events which were to follow. Thus, the final
scene of the play anticipates the great drama which was to
take a more precise form after the end of the second World
War, and whose denouement we today are still unable to
foresee. I might note in passing that the play, performed for
the first time in Paris in 1937, was presented by the students
of the University of Brussels in 1949, as I recall, and it seemed
so close to present-day issues that many were surprised to
learn that it had been written before the war.

Eustache Soreau, as I have said, belonged to a Parisian family
of very modest means. An excellent and hard-working student, he has won scholarships, distinguished himself in exam-
inations and *concours,* and is presently teaching in a Paris

lycée. He has been the tutor of a wealthy politician's son and
has married his pupil's sister, Béatrice Durand Fresnel. His
father-in-law, who congratulates himself on having given his
daughter to an impecunious young man, has used his political
influence to advance Soreau's academic career. So Eustache
has been lucky. He acknowledges the fact and even speaks
of it repeatedly with a feeling of bitterness verging on exasperation. An acquaintance of his, Gertrude Heuzard, a girl
who was a militant worker with him in the ranks of the
Socialist party and who lost her teaching position for having
carried her revolutionary propaganda into the classroom, never
stops showing Eustache, by insinuations and caustic allusions,
that she looks upon him as a turncoat, hating him for allowing
himself to become a bourgeois. By marrying into a rich family,
he has betrayed the class to which he belonged—the working
class. Eustache's mother, on the other hand, a good but somewhat vulgar woman, whose mental capacity is that of a con-
cierge or a charwoman, treats her daughter-in-law with almost servile respect, which makes Eustache angry. He is
hypersensitive; his bad conscience gnaws at him, as evidenced
by his violent outbursts whenever he expresses his anti-Fascist
convictions. I was very much interested in showing that success—a certain kind of success—may become a source of
resentment. Similarly, a friend of mine, recently returned
from countries in Dark Africa formerly belonging to the
French Union, told me that the natives there appeared to her
deprived of a revolution, frustrated and bitter because they
had received as a gift what apparently they would have pre-
ferred to snatch, like spoils after a battle.

Sometime before, while a lecturer at the University of
Marburg, Eustache had known a young German, Werner
Schnee, who had become his friend. The latter is a singer of
lieder, an artist capable of interpreting with delicacy and
depth the great German Romantic composers. But his accom-
panist, Rudolf Schonthal, who is a Jew, has received shameful

treatment at the hands of the Nazis and has been forced to leave Germany. In a gesture of solidarity, Werner also has left his native country, to the great displeasure of his wife Gisela, who claims she is not interested in politics any more than she is interested in "that ugly Jew with the protruding ears." The Soreaus have opened their home to Werner and his wife. The young singer has just come back from Switzerland where his friend Rudolf is dying, a victim of Nazi cruelty.

But cohabitation will bring out into the open the latent hostility between Eustache and Werner.

Every opinion and every judgment of Eustache Soreau is inspired by his desire to remain in line with a certain class ideology. And indeed his constant desire not to betray the social milieu of his birth may appear a noble thing in principle. But it will soon be discovered that this preoccupation is vitiated, as it were, by his bad conscience. Toward Béatrice whom he loves, however, and who has deep affection for him, his conduct is unjust and almost hateful; he blames her for supporting the cause of the privileged bourgeoisie which he despises. But, though probably not blind to her parents' shortcomings, she has no desire to break her ties with them. Between her family and her husband she tries to be a steadying influence in a rapidly worsening situation. With a clearsightedness not unmixed with deep compassion she follows the progress of the sort of moral disease from which Eustache is suffering: a guilty conscience.

Werner Schnee, by leaving his homeland, has shown his horror of Hitlerism; yet for his part, he wishes to remain independent of all parties, whatever they may be. Eustache reproaches him for not associating with the other German political refugees, but it is because he does not wish to develop a refugee mentality, which would be distasteful to him as a kind of uniform like any other. Eustache accuses him of being an individualist. But this is only a label, and Werner dislikes all labels. Above all, he intends to remain a man—a word

which grates on Eustache's nerves. We have here a fundamental point. Werner despises what he calls ideology. He
sees that if his friend likes Beethoven, it is because he ascribes
to the German composer a democratic ideology very similar
to his own. Now, whatever Beethoven's political opinions may
have been, they have nothing to do with his genius, which is
all that matters. For his genius is an integral part of his humanity—that is to say, his way of touching the hearts of all
men. It is in this respect that he is universal. In the eyes of
Werner, however, the partisan spirit he finds in Eustache is
exactly the opposite of this kind of universality. Werner accuses him of judging others, not on their intrinsic qualities
but according to the category into which they fall. Needless
to say, Eustache reacts vigorously to the way in which Werner
judges him, and hostility grows between the two men. What
makes it worse is the fact that Eustache vaguely feels his
wife's sympathy for Werner and his jealousy is aroused.
Finally Eustache commits a shameful act. Werner has told
him in the strictest confidence that an emissary from the Hitler
government has come to him with a proposal that he return
to Germany where he would be offered an engagement in
an opera house on condition that he give his allegiance to
the political regime. He has refused, of course. He would
have disgraced himself by accepting such an offer. Yet he
has refrained from telling his wife Gisela about it; she would
not have understood. Yielding to some shameful impulse,
Eustache discloses to the young woman the secret entrusted
to him by Werner. She flies into a rage when she learns that
they could have returned to Germany. They separate, and
the wife eventually joins a German baron who has been
courting her for some time and with whom she will be able
to return home without any difficulty.

Thus Eustache, always obsessed by the idea of treason,
treason to his class—that is, to an entity—betrays a real human
being, one he used to call his friend. Werner is generous

enough to give his wife the little money he has left; he will soon be reduced to poverty. From every side, to be sure, he receives invitations, because he has the gift of arousing sympathy. But he refuses to make use of this gift to derive material advantage from it. A scruple the nature of which he himself is unable to understand prevents him from drawing any profit from the ability he has of touching men's hearts, as if he, too, had fallen a prey to a *guilty conscience,* to such an extent that he wonders if in a certain mysterious way he has not been tainted by Eustache. However, this guilty conscience prompts him to do something heroic, a thing that some will call the act of a madman. He, too, is going to return to Germany, but without the passport offered by Hitler's henchmen. He knows from now on what his fate will be: he will be arrested, and this is what he wants because he suddenly realizes that this gift, this favor or grace, which has been granted to him, he may find useful in helping the unfortunate political prisoners with whom he will mingle. Here let us understand clearly that there can be no question for him of political affiliation since he will continue to the end to be a nonpolitical man. What counts for him is the fact that those political prisoners are unfortunate, innocent people who are being shamefully treated. He will bring to them at least the benefit of his presence, of the music that lives in him and that can be bestowed as charity. There is also another reason for this decision: Werner has come to realize that Eustache was right in suspecting him and that, in fact, he is in love with Béatrice. And as the latter in turn has serious grievances against Eustache, since out of spite he has finally become the lover of the bitter and resentful Gertrude, Werner feels that if he remained in France, neither she nor even he himself could resist temptation. By his decision to return to Germany under the conditions I mentioned, he sets up before her an insurmountable obstacle. And this is what he explains to Béatrice in the last scene of the play—to Béatrice, who finds it difficult to rise with him to such heights. More than that, his leaving under such circumstances appears to her as a kind of suicide. "Not in the least," Werner objects, "suicide is a crime . . . I am simply putting myself at the disposal . . ." "Of what?" asks Béatrice. "Of the cause? Of the revolution?" "I am not interested in the cause," he says emphatically, "I am interested in men." And as he senses that perhaps Béatrice is going to weaken and abandon to his fate the husband she despises, he appeals to her: "You cannot leave him. You must always remember that you are the wife of a pauper . . . Poverty is not lack of money or lack of success. Eustache has had money, he has had success. He has remained poor and grown poorer still. No doubt he will never be cured of his poverty. This is the greatest evil of our time; it spreads like a plague. No physician has yet been found to treat it. It cannot even be diagnosed. Perhaps the artist will be spared, even if he starves. And also the true believer who can pray . . . All other people are in danger."

Béatrice. You ask me to live with a leper.
Werner. Leper colonies are going to multiply here on earth, I fear. To very few people will grace be granted to live there, knowing they are among lepers and yet not finding them repulsive. Much more than grace, they will need a viaticum to sustain them on their way.
Béatrice. I am not brave enough, Werner, I assure you.
Werner. You will think of me, as I think of Rudolf. Later on I shall be in you a living presence, as Rudolf still is in me. You will remember then what I told you here a few weeks ago. If there were only the living, Béatrice . . .[2]

The words he spoke were these: "If there were only the living, I think life on this earth would be quite impossible."

But all this calls for a commentary which penetrates to the core of what I wish to make clear in the course of this book: what *is* this poverty which is neither lack of money nor lack

[2] *Le Dard*, Act III, scene viii.

of success and which, we are told, is going to spread like leprosy? It might be said, I think, that it is the spirit of abstraction which finds in our own day—and we must not hesitate to say so—its most terrifying though not its only incarnation in communism. But this spirit of abstraction cannot be separated from a certain lack of love, and by this I mean the inability to treat a human being as a human being, and for this human being the substituting of a certain idea, a certain abstract designation. The leper colonies which are going to multiply on earth (let me recall that this was written in 1936) are the popular democracies, to the extent that they are committed to the spirit of abstraction in its Marxist form. But we must hasten to add that any technocracy, even if it belongs to the capitalist system, can be guilty of the same fundamental error. When it goes so far as to consider the individual within the framework of society as a mere unit of production and to judge his worth only in terms of productivity, it also tends to create communities of lepers, however attractive their outward aspect may be. When, for example, I see huge buildings being erected on the outskirts of Paris, impersonal, merciless structures, not for human beings to dwell in (for "to dwell" still has a human connotation) but to be "incorporated into," I have the immediate and almost physical feeling of this universal threat which today weighs upon human beings, so that, after passing through these suburbs where everything changes before our eyes at such amazing speed, I have even gone so far as to say that it was already the setting up of a communist society.

Here, the reader may very well raise an objection to the abrupt and arbitrary manner in which his attention has been diverted from the very particular cases which I have treated in my plays to a wholly general situation which refuses to be confined within the limits of such specific cases. He may well question, for example, what possible connection there is between a guilty conscience and technocracy. Undoubtedly, this would appear to be a strong objection; but I shall say only that anyone who raises the objection places himself on a plane which is, as a matter of fact, altogether different from mine, not only with respect to my plays, but also with respect to the existential philosophy which I have tried to develop since I began my independent thinking.

It is of course obvious that if one remains in the realm of notions, it is quite impossible to extract from an idea such as that of technocracy or, for that matter, of any social regime considered in terms of its distinctive characteristics, anything resembling what I have called a guilty conscience. But what matters to me is not technocracy taken in itself, since it is still, after all, an abstraction, but rather what it tends to do to the individuals who will have to live under it. Moreover—and this is of the utmost importance—the world we live in, which is also the world of my plays, is one in which technocracy does not reign supreme. Technocracy is felt as a distant threat, and at the same time as a spirit tending more and more to inform life. A character like Eustache cannot be separated from this context, namely, that of a changing society in which the class struggle as Marx had conceived of it, within the framework of a society moving towards industrialization (such as it appeared to that remarkable observer), the class struggle, let me repeat, tends to be replaced by very different relations, infinitely more subtle and less rigid springing from the fact that a certain section of the bourgeoisie joined the proletariat and that a very large portion of the proletariat formed a bourgeois class. Now if I were asked why I made Werner Schnee a singer—Werner, a man struggling for the universal against the masses—I would answer that my motives for that choice became apparent to me a posteriori, and always for the same reason, because I did not pass from the abstract idea to the concrete, but rather the reverse. A singer like

Werner Schnee is, essentially, an unselfish, dedicated person, since the task to which he has devoted his life consists in making available to others the work of the great creative artists: Werner is a mediator, as any instrumentalist would be, but mediation here is more evident and vital than in any other case, because the voice is part of the human being, much more so than an instrument such as a violin or a piano. It could also be said that the spiritual climate of Werner is admiration. The question for him is to use this power within him to serve what he admires and, in effect, to make it admirable to listeners—but, needless to say, not just *any* listeners. In this domain there is no room for just *anybody*, since there are people to whom an art will always remain something alien—because of a *disgrace* whose nature and significance actually escape us. It is a fact that we simply have to accept. And the existence of these "outsiders," or, more exactly, these Boeotians, does not detract from the universality of the message, for this universality, in terms of logic, must be conceived not in extension but only in comprehension. In an interpreter like Werner Schnee, the self, it would seem, tends to be absorbed in the inspired act of serving the beautiful work of art, which does not mean, of course, that vanity can be excluded from it. Such is the nature of the human being that this vanity can force its way in anywhere, as a kind of corrosion. But we can safely say that the conditions leading to a perfect interpretation tend in some way to preclude this intervention. This is most certainly true in the case of Werner Schnee, and the sympathetic feeling he inspires in those around him can surely be ascribed to the fact that he exists as little as possible for himself. In that, by the way, he may be likened to the believer. We may recall Werner's words to Béatrice quoted earlier: the artist will probably be safe from this disease of poverty as well as the true believer who can pray. In either case, salvation comes from transcendence, even if, here and there, it takes on very different aspects; and this transcendency, as we shall see more and more clearly, is closely related to universality.

It may be necessary here to return to what I meant by admiration. It is not enough to say that it has been of tremendous importance in my own life, and that, for me, the inability to admire is the supreme misfortune. I have always felt that admiration was of the same order as creation, that undoubtedly it was even a sort of merciful dispensation by which those who have been denied the gift of creating visible things can nevertheless reach the level on which the creative spirit reveals itself. The idea of a relationship between admiration and creation may be surprising at first, because it would seem that people tend to confuse creation and production. Yet it could be said, generally speaking, that any production depends on a technique and that creation, on the contrary, is of a meta-technical order. This may seem at first a purely verbal distinction. But what I have tried to show is that in reality any creation is a response to a call received, and it is receptivity that we should stress here while pointing out that a serious error is made whenever receptivity and passivity are confused, as it seems to me they are in Kant, for example. This idea, which I discussed for the first time in a study included later in the volume entitled *Du refus à l'invocation*, belongs therefore to approximately the same period as *Le Dard*, and the relationship is as clear as can be between *Le Monde cassé* and *Position et approches concrètes*. I shall quote a passage from this essay which is directly related to the idea of active or creative receptivity:

We already find in the process of acquiring knowledge the paradox which is at the heart of creation proper, but this paradox may perhaps be more easily detected in the artist than in the areas where knowledge is elaborated and where the pragmatic in all its forms comes to cover up the initial mystery of the *naissance-au-réel* (becoming aware of the real) whose depth is essentially unfathomable. The artist appears to himself as sustained by the very thing he tries to incarnate. Thus in him the identification of receiving and giving is finally effected. But this can be achieved only in his own particular sphere corresponding in this register to the *area* such as I described it when I analyzed the *chez soi*. There is every reason to believe that there is no difference of nature but merely a difference of power between the ability to feel and the ability to create; both presuppose not only the existence of a *soi*, but of a world in which the *soi* recognizes itself, exercises and spreads itself; a world in between the closed and the open, between *having* and *being*, and of which my body appears necessarily the symbol or the materialized nucleus. But we are entitled to suppose that we are grossly deceived by appearances in our hypostasis when we treat as independent, circumscribed reality what may be only the emergence of some measureless kingdom whose submerged regions and underwater ramifications can be sighted only accidentally and by sudden illuminations. Might not the very fact of living, in the full sense we give the word when we speak of our own life, of human life, imply for one who would go to the heart of the matter, the existence of a metaphysical Atlantis, unexplorable by definition, but whose presence actually gives our own experience its dimension, its value, and its mysterious quality? [3]

It would be appropriate, of course, in the perspective we have adopted here, to state more explicitly what was treated in this passage in allusive and metaphorical terms. The difficulty is, however, that what we are considering could not in all likelihood be conceptualized without contradiction. For the concepts can be formed only from the sphere which lies, as I have said, between having and being. And it could be said that thought, when it comes to these obscure shores, uses a method of approach entirely different from the one it uses when it applies itself to knowing or even to understanding something. I need hardly say that here we find again, though at a deeper level of experience, what has been said earlier about participation. But what I wish to emphasize is that a careful examination of active receptivity can help us formu-

[3] *Du refus à l'invocation*, pp. 123–124.

late our conception of man and of what we have called human dignity. Indeed, the time has come to deal squarely with this notion of dignity.

We must admit that in current phraseology what is called the dignity of the human being is described in terms of Kantism (here, by the way, reduced to its simplest expression). I refer to the idea according to which the inalienable value of man lies in the fact that he is a rational being, that stress is placed on his faculty of understanding and comprehending the intelligible order of the world, or rather on his faculty of conforming to certain maxims considered as universally valid. To my mind, there can be no question of challenging the legitimate value of such an interpretation. Yet, at the same time, it seems to me difficult to deny that during the last hundred years or so this rationalism, respectable as it may be, has lost much of what can be termed its vitality, as if it had gradually loosened its hold on men's minds. And the development of the philosophy of existence in its various aspects, and also, we might add, of the philosophy of life espoused by Bergson and his followers, could not be understood without this increasing lack of interest in a form of thought threatened by the dangers of formalism.

It is my own profound belief that we cannot succeed in preserving the mysterious principle at the heart of human dignity unless we succeed in making explicit the properly sacral quality peculiar to it, a quality which will appear all the more clearly when we consider the human being in his nudity and weakness—the human being as helpless as the child, the old man, or the pauper. Here we should consider a paradox which appears at first glance to be extremely embarrassing.

Do we not run the risk, as a rule, of letting ourselves be deceived by what I would like to call a decorative conception of dignity—and the word "dignity" here is significant—which we more or less confuse with the display of pomp that usually accompanies power? It is considered advisable, for example,

to surround the judicial power with appearances and conditions likely to command respect, or, if one prefers, to put a
certain distance between men entrusted with high duties and
ordinary people. It would be an error, certainly—perhaps
even an aberration—to deny the necessity of enhancing, even
by artificial means, the value of certain institutions when these
assume, in any degree whatever, the character of a sacerdotal
function. But at the same time there is always the fear that,
humanly speaking, this pomp may conceal only emptiness and
deceit—and if so, it can be truthfully said it turns against
itself, as it were, and finally in the eyes of the critical observer
deals a crushing blow to its own authority. This remains true
even if we leave aside such things as uniforms or pompous
display to consider only the attitudes, the solemn tone of voice,
the gestures: these, as often as not, may arouse in the one
who remains "outside" a questioning attitude which can easily
turn into challenge and revolt.

It is in this line of existential thought that rationalism, it
seems to me, shows its weakness, a weakness that the men of
the present day can hardly fail to notice. It is as if we had
become more and more aware of the fact that reason may
become sham and parody. But considerations of another kind
point in the same direction: it can be said that our times will
have witnessed what I might readily term a gradual seculariza-
tion of reason, a functional treatment tending more and more
to reduce reason to a series of technical operations depending
on a descriptive science. Around it there is hardly anything
left of the aura which still accompanied the word *Vernunft*,
for example, for Kant and his followers. I do not claim, however, that this process of reduction can ever become exhaustive
enough to leave nothing deserving attention or even respect;
I am in my own mind deeply convinced of the contrary.
But I doubt that the language of the traditional rationalist
philosophy, as it was in the past, is capable of conveying to
the mind of modern man this reality which one might be

tempted to call residual, and which undoubtedly must be described as both immediate and secret. These two words seem to contradict each other, but the contradiction, if we pause to reflect, appears inherent in what we call the sacred.

The phenomenologist, Emmanuel Lévinas, in a recent treatise entitled *Totalité et infini,*[4] showed, I think, great insight in this, by stressing the irreducible originality of what he calls the "face to face," that is to say, how the other person's face appears to me. He thinks—and I am strongly tempted to go along with him in this—that the otherness we speak of here can in no way be reduced to the one which a dialectic of the Hegelian type can, through conflict, finally reduce to identity. Here, otherness presents a consistency which is wholly lacking in the world of objects or objectifiable data. I shall not examine here the way in which Emmanuel Lévinas tries to avoid the pluralism such a position may seem to imply. It is rather surprising that in designating a person who is "other" but who, at the same time, presents himself to me to be not only confronted but greeted, he does not use the term which seems to me the only adequate one—"neighbor." We should note that this word takes its full meaning only when preceded by the possessive adjective, the possessive in this case no longer being used to claim ownership.

It goes without saying that here again we find—doubtless at a deeper level of experience—what has been said earlier of the vocative "thou." It is in a philosophy centered on the second person that the words "my neighbor" come to have meaning.

It is apparent, on the other hand, that from the experience implicit in the words "my neighbor" we are drawn almost imperceptibly to the affirmation of a fraternity. But here we come to an important point which we have no right to overlook. In principle I can call "my brothers" only those born of the same father as I. Brotherhood, or fraternity, implies a

[4] The Hague: Martinus Nijhoff, 1961.

common sonship. And everything leads one to think that the first French revolutionists, when they laid at the very foundation of the Declaration of the Rights of Man, liberty, equality and fraternity—in their eyes an indivisible unit—were actuated by an underlying deism which was later to be questioned. It may seem paradoxical that the inscription "Liberty, Equality, Fraternity" appears on all public buildings in an officially "laique" country where, for a long time, the belief in a God who is Father of all men has been purely a matter of choice. Under these conditions, fraternity has become nothing more than an "as if": men must behave toward one another *as if* they were brothers. What we see here is only a vague aspiration or perhaps a dim nostalgic feeling for a past era when fraternity was an article of faith. The situation respecting equality is quite different, since this word expresses an exigency which tends to be more and more institutionalized, considerably more attention being given, incidentally, to rights than to duties and obligations. But a very important question can be raised here, one which has been in my mind since the end of the second World War and which has also been approached, though in an indirect manner, by an Austrian who has been residing in the United States since the last war and has taught in American universities. I refer to Count Kühnelt-Leddihn and to his book, *Liberty or Equality*.[5] It is, of course, on the conjunction *or* that the stress is placed. As for me, without knowing anything at that time of the writings of Count Kühnelt-Leddihn, I had, for the first time in Lisbon in 1949, attempted to show that, contrary to the belief of the men of 1789 and their innumerable followers, there would appear to exist between equality and fraternity a secret opposition connected with the fact that these two exigencies stem from two different sources. As I have already noted, equality is essentially the claiming of something; it is, in the fullest sense of

[5] Erik Maria von Kühnelt-Leddihn, *Liberty or Equality: The Challenge of Our Time*, ed. John P. Hughes (London: Hollis & Carter, 1952).

the word, ego-centric. I am your equal, his equal, or their equal.
Probing further, we would not have any difficulty in finding,
after Nietzsche and Scheler, the presence of resentment at
the heart of equality. It must, of course, be added that this
presence, which is not, and in a sense cannot, be ascertained,
remains hidden under a rational or pseudo-rational camou-
flage. There is no reason why I should not be your equal;
it would be even irrational to admit that I am not.

One would have to show further by what processes one
passes from evident equality in certain rights to equality that
is much less evident in all rights, to the supposed equality of
the subjects themselves, this equality of all men—supposing
the word has a meaning, which is exceedingly doubtful—
justifying the equality of rights.

But with fraternity, it seems to me, the case is very different.
Unlike equality, fraternity is essentially hetero-centric: you
are my brother, I recognize you as such, I greet you as my
brother. It is certainly evident that the reverse is possible
here. It may happen, if I am wronged by you, that I have
to remind you reproachfully that, after all, I am your brother.
But this is only a derived case. And, further, it is very likely
that in such an event I would address these words of blame
to you in the name of my rights trampled upon by *you*—that
is, in the name of equality much more than of fraternity. But
if we focus our attention on the act of expansive recognition
forming the basis of fraternity, it will be seen as a spontaneous
movement exactly the reverse of the claim implied in equality:
you are my brother and, because you are my brother, I re-
joice not only in anything good which may happen to you but
also in acknowledging the ways in which you are superior
to me. Why should I feel the need of being your equal? We
are brothers through all our dissimilarities, and why should
these dissimilarities not imply inequalities in your favor—
surely I shall not say to my detriment—for, since we are
brothers, it is exactly as if the radiance emanating from your

gifts, acts, and works were reflected on me. This I shall express perhaps if I say very simply: "I am proud of you," which indeed would be meaningless, even impossible, if I were intent on being or on showing myself your equal.

But here I should close what may well be regarded as a long parenthesis: everything we have said leads us to think that if human dignity can today be fully recognized without our necessarily falling into the old groove of abstract rationalism, it is on condition that we place ourselves in the perspective of fraternity and not of equalitarianism. Here I must return to a thought I may have conveyed earlier in this discussion. I think it would be wrong, or at any rate unwise, to claim that human dignity is the concern only of those, whatever their form of worship may be, who explicitly recognize God as Father of all men, this dignity appearing as the very mark of the *imago dei*. Or, more exactly, I feel that such a position could not be accepted purely and simply, although there cannot be any question of explicitly rejecting it. To accept it would be to make light of the fact that an unbeliever —I do not say an atheist, since the term does not fit in this context—may, in fact, have a keen and exacting sense of human dignity and give in his actions the most irrefutable proof of it. I do not have in mind particularly those who are against injustice and oppression in speech only, for such a verbal protest is of doubtful value, except when it involves risks for the one who formulates it. What I am thinking of, rather, is an active interest in the oppressed, whoever they may be. And in practice this interest does imply the consciousness of a fraternal relationship with those very people who are to be defended. Shall we say that those unbelievers entertain, in spite of everything, a belief in God as a father, a belief which remains concealed under their opinions as free-thinkers? In this connection, I myself have dwelt on the important fact that each of us can be mistaken about what he thinks he believes and what he actually believes. And, if this is so, then belief is really a mode of being and can by no means be likened to an opinion, that is, to something one possesses.

I feel, however, that one should not go so far as to interpret this in an apologetic sense. As for the unbeliever, I should prefer to say this: insofar as he truly possesses the militant character I have just described, he has an active and even poignant experience of the mystery inherent in the human condition and in everything in it which is hazardous, precarious, and, at the same time, tragic. And what we discover in this line of thought is compassion, in the strongest sense of the word, and consequently to the degree that it implies in the person who feels it nothing at all resembling a feeling of superiority. This would amount to saying, then, that dignity must be sought at the antipodes of pretension and rather on the side of weakness. Here again, as I have done so often, I shall quote the words of one of my characters, Arnaud, at the end of *Les Cœurs avides*. His father is a man who seems to be always speaking "to the gallery," in a dogmatic and somewhat solemn manner and, as a result, he himself is the only one deceived by this verbal pomposity intended to impress his audience. In this final scene, he yields to weariness and dozes off. His son, Arnaud, a devout Christian, in whom the spirit of a child still lives, meditates before the sleeping old man: "It won't be long now," he says to himself, "before all these sentences he has been delighting in will be lost in silence. This affectation he takes so seriously will fall from him. He will remain here alone, weak and defenseless, like a child overcome by sleep and still clasping his toy to his breast. When in the presence of the living man who rants and raves, if only we could imagine him lying cold in death tomorrow."

Here we have a contrast which I find especially illuminating for the thought I have tried to bring out in this chapter—the contrast between an affected dignity which, because of its affectation, becomes the very antithesis of dignity, and the inalienable dignity inherent in the condemnation which is the fate of every man from the very fact of his birth. And here lies a paradox whose meaning deserves to be clarified.

At first sight, one might be tempted to say that the fact of man's mortality makes not only his acts but also his being appear ridiculously insignificant. And we must admit that contemporary man is only too prone to follow this line of thought. Now the moment the insignificance of the individual is declared, the way is paved for all forms of tyranny and especially for those which operate today behind a screen of democratic phraseology. But the remarkable thing is that this way is not the only one, and even more remarkable is the fact that within us something builds up to resist this disintegration and downward course. We shall have to determine more clearly and precisely the significance and nature of this resistance, but even now it should be sufficiently clear that this resistance is founded, not on the affirmation of the self and the pretensions it exudes, but on a stronger consciousness of the living tie which unites all men.

VIII ◄

Mortality, Hope, and Freedom

THE preceding chapter closed with the evocation of a
choice and the enunciation of a paradox. There is a
temptation which seems for many men of our time to be
almost irresistible to argue from the fact of man's mortality
that he is negligible as an individual, and to transfer to the
collective and to society that regard of which he has been
judged positively unworthy. But to reason in this way is to
follow a road which leads to tyranny and to servitude. Now
the paradox which we considered briefly in the preceding
chapter is that we can, on the contrary, find in man's finitude
itself the principle of his essential dignity. How is this possible? We have to take as a point of departure the fact that
man is the only being known to us who knows himself to
be mortal. Moreover, in the perspective we have adopted this
fact reveals that man transcends the society to which a certain
type of "reason" pretends to sacrifice him: for this very
society, if it has a destiny, is not conscious of it, is incapable
of having a conception of it, and *a fortiori* of mastering it. In
the final reckoning, then, the priority rests with the individual.

In any case, we must not fail to note that the fact of this
knowledge of one's own mortality involves the same in-
determinateness with regard to value that I drew attention
to earlier: from this ambiguous situation we can emerge only

on condition that we pass beyond the limits of the ego. In the text of *Les Cœurs avides* which I have cited, Arnaud was meditating not on his own mortality, but on that of his father. And this meditation was suffused with a compassion which was also a form of piety. It is precisely the nature of this piety which is to be accounted for, without, however, assuming that it can be reduced to something simpler and "self-evident" in the Cartesian sense.

I believe that our first obligation is resolutely to avoid the reductionist interpretation which would see in this piety a weakened and faded survival of superstitious fears. Of course, such attempts at derivation will always be possible, but they would all be open to the central objection that almost inevitably applies to any claim that "such and such is *nothing but* this or that" in other words, to the denial of the distinctive quality of a given experience in the name of genetic considerations. The truth would seem to be rather that piety toward the dead, or toward those whose death we anticipate, fulfills a demand for compensation, which pertains perhaps to a secret modality of justice. Everything happens as if the pious man—and I take this adjective in the most nonconfessional sense—felt called upon to oppose to this process of deterioration, operating on the level of corruptible flesh, an inverse movement directed upward, or one might say towards exaltation, had that word not lost its noble and etymological connotation. But here we must probe still deeper. What takes place—and that usually beyond the reach of explicit formulation—is the confidence that in death one's being will raise itself to an integrity which life lived would perhaps not have allowed it, because of life's perpetually dispersed, tortured, and torn character. The famous line of Mallarmé, "Tel qu'en lui-même enfin l'éternité le change," [1] happily renders this accession to eternity.

It is true that what is sometimes disclosed at the end of a

---

[1] "As eternity at last gives him back to himself." (Tr.)

life is its fundamental nullity, its inanity, or, what is even
worse than nothingness, a perverted will embodied in a chain
of actions, a will to destroy everything of man's which makes
for communication and peace. But it seems to me that it would
always be difficult to hold to such a judgment; inevitably,
something comes to attenuate its force and to refocus it into
a question. For this same being who seemed to have willed
evil was either deprived of love, in which case it is as if at the
close of his existence he himself became accuser, or else he
was loved, and this love to which he could not respond cannot help but take on the character of an intercession. But it
is true that this word "intercession" can have meaning only
if it is unspoken, and if the intersubjective consciousness refuses to admit or, *a fortiori*, to proclaim the finality of death.
This is not the place to enter directly into the complex and
involved argument which I have elsewhere devoted to the
problem of survival, and which I have already touched upon
in connection with *L'Iconoclaste*. Here I would draw attention to just one or two points:

To begin with, it seems to me that whatever our religious
or agnostic position we have to reject any negativist dogmatism, which is usually founded on a superannuated scientism.
Furthermore, we must acknowledge that, contrary to the
claim of societies under the domination of an official atheism,
which allow themselves to be ruled by the logic of that same
atheism, the exclusion of human life from any extension into
the realm of the invisible is by no means reflected in a greater
respect for human life or a more solicitous treatment of it;
nor has it benefited from the fact that theoretically it is regarded as a good whose loss is irretrievable. I am rather inclined to think that in the societies in question a devaluation
of life has come about in the sense that one might speak of a
currency devaluation. Wars and revolutions with their fearful
consumption of human lives have had such an effect. I recall
the comment of a well-known general, made in the presence

of a relative of mine who was a General Staff Officer, on the day after a bloody offensive action during the first World War: "Men are replaceable." Scandalous, and even sacrilegious words, for in fact a human individual is precisely *that which is not replaceable*. But it must be emphasized that our time, more than any other, has succeeded in introducing a merchandising distinction between "wholesale" and "retail" into a domain from which it should have been forever excluded. But that is one consequence among many others of a materialism that in our time pervades not only our opinions but our way of life, and which, with an inconsistency that does no honor to human nature, is even coexistent in some people— I would not say with authentic religious beliefs, but with the ghosts of such beliefs.

In the third place—but this is an observation of a different order from the foregoing—I think we must be on guard against a religious predisposition which, in the name of more or less correctly interpreted revealed texts, rejects a priori a metaphysical conception which has to do with the beyond. The Protestant theologian Jean Hering has justly observed that on the one hand it is not the function of the theologian to take sides for or against reincarnation, which depends on a mode of knowledge that is wholly foreign to theology, but that on the other, a fundamental dogma like that of the resurrection of the body belongs to a quite special domain, to which the non-theologian has no access.[2] For my own part, I have always thought that the doctrine of reincarnation deserved much more attentive study than it has generally received from philosophers, and that it was possible for empirical facts to be uncovered which would make it appear to be a quite plausible hypothesis.[3]

If I feel obliged to introduce these few remarks here, it

[2] Jean Hering, *Revue d'histoire et de philosophie religieuses* (University of Strasbourg, 1960), pp. 338–348.

[3] See the two articles by Ian Stevenson, M. D., in *Journal of the American Society for Psychical Research* (April 1960).

is because it seems to me necessary to appraise the thickness
of the concrete wall within which man today tends increasingly to enclose himself—a wall which is more and more
impenetrable to all the premonitions and intimations of a
spiritual counterpoise to that Luciferian solitude to which
man seems self-condemned.

The objection will doubtless be raised that theosophical and
spiritualist societies can be found in plenty whose professed
aims are to maintain or re-establish such communication between man and the next world. I am mindful of it, and am
indeed in regular contact with American and English societies
for parapsychological research, where serious and valuable
work is unquestionably being done. But we must remember
that in this sphere critical research encounters especially difficult conditions, for it operates in a realm where truth and
error are inextricably intertwined. We should note especially
that this research has a marginal character with respect to
the development of science proper. Among French scientists,
and among the philosophers as well, there is an extraordinary
aversion to acknowledging such solidly established phenomena
as telepathy and mind reading, solely because these phenomena
run counter to certain unexamined postulates. Thus, a rationalist like Alain, in an article published some thirty years ago,
made what seemed to me the scandalous observation that even
if parapsychological phenomena *were* taking place somewhere,
he would take good care not to be present. What was being
upheld here was a notion of intelligence as a sort of customs
inspector, for it was in fact a species of contraband that was
being excluded. I have always opposed such an attitude of
mind, and it is perhaps at this point that we might enlist that
adventurous disposition I evoked in my first chapter.

I must beg the reader's indulgence for the digressive and
perhaps random character of these comments, touching upon
the connection—which in my view is a valid one, though
difficult to specify—between parapsychological research and

the refusal to dogmatize about the nature of death, even if that refusal cannot take the form of a positive and unqualified affirmation of survival.

But, generally speaking, philosophers, up to the present time, have paid almost no attention to certain structural characteristics of the human being which allow for the insertion of freedom into the fabric of our existence. Once more, unless one is the champion of a scientific materialism which seems to be plainly dated, I do not see how it can be seriously maintained that survival after death is purely and simply unthinkable. A margin of incertitude remains, and it is open to reflection as an aspect of the mystery involved in our destiny. And surely it would be equally wrong to regard this margin as fixed and constant, and therefore independent of the ways in which we tend to orient our existence in this world. It is plain that the more each one of us takes himself for a center, considering others only in relation to himself, the more the idea of the beyond will be emptied of all meaning, for this world beyond will then appear as a senseless prolongation. That is its character in a perspective like Sartre's where "the other" is thought of primarily as a threat to my integrity, or, in other words, my self-sufficiency. On the contrary, the more the other, or others, will have become an integral part of my experience, the more I will be led to recognize their irreducible value as well as the difficulty *for us* of achieving a lasting harmony here below; and the more necessary it will be to conceive a mode of existence which is different from the one we have known, and which will lead us toward the real and *pleromatic* unity where we will be all in all.

I am by no means underestimating the force of the objection which is unfailingly provoked by such an assertion. It will be ascribed to the kind of wishful thinking which rigorous reflection is obliged to reject.

But it is at this juncture that the reflections on hope which I was led to develop in the midst of the second World War become relevant. I took as my point of departure the idea that desire and hope must be carefully distinguished, and that Spinoza in particular erred in identifying them. I had already observed in *Positions et approches concrètes* that the opposition is not, as Spinoza said, between fear and hope, but rather between fear and desire, and I added that the negative correlative of hope is to adopt the perspective of the worst, as the defeatist does, for example. But ten years after this book was written I tried in a more searching way to cast light on some of the fundamental characteristics of hope, basing my reflection on the situation which was ours as Frenchmen, namely, defeat and oppression by the enemy, or, more plainly still, the situation of prisoners awaiting liberation. What was revealed to me then, in a *syneidesis* like those to which I referred earlier, is that hope is always tied to an experience of captivity: "But I appear to myself as captive if I am conscious not only of being thrown into a situation, but engaged by it—under external constraint—in a mode of existence which carries with it restrictions of all kinds on my own action . . . Such a situation makes it impossible for me to rise to an experienced plenitude either of feeling or of thought." But what I realize correlatively is that the subject of "I hope" is not reducible to the ego which is the subject of desire, or, in other words, that the subject of "I hope" excludes all claims. Such claims are in a certain way present in optimism, as found in someone who, confronted with a tragic situation, declares in the name of a wisdom to which he apparently lays claim, "I tell you that things will work out"—while his defeatist interlocutor will say with the same assurance, "Well, I say that nothing will work out and the worst will happen." It is as if hope were situated in another dimension of which it could be said that it is that of humility and patience, a patience which is perhaps a profound and secret characteristic of life. If then we say, as we must, that hope is the act by which the temptation to despair is actively overcome, we must add that this victory is not necessarily accompanied by a feeling of effort; it is even linked to relaxation rather than to tension. But it should be stressed that this relaxation is not, and must not be, a slackening. This is one of the points on which I have been most insistent, especially with respect to the conception that we should have of the will. A type of stoicism, which has perhaps been essentially distorted by the expression given it in poets such as Lucanus and Corneille, seems to me to have contributed most unfortunately to the distortion of the reality here in question. I mentioned patience above, but it is obvious that this is the very opposite of passivity. We must in fact beware of falling prey to the same confusion to which I have drawn attention in connection with receptivity. As regards hope, nothing could be more mistaken than to see it as a kind of inactive hovering over an event which is expected to come to pass all by itself. It is indeed true that hope or patience can sink to the level where a sense of ease becomes mere slackening. I might quote here a few lines from "Phénoménologie de l'espérance," in *Homo Viator*.[4] I was answering the objection that might be made to the assertion that patience is generally operative in a person—a child, or someone who is sick, for example—while hope operates with respect to a situation which does not seem capable of being personalized:

> On reflection, the gap nonetheless tends to narrow, possibly because I have or have not hope in the being for whom I bear responsibility, and one may justifiably ask oneself whether "I have hope in thee" is not really the most authentic form of the verb "I hope." But this does not exhaust the matter; the nature of the test is revealed in its effect on me, in the way it impinges on my being, insofar as it leaves me open to a permanent alteration. So it is that illness, for example, may make me into that deformed being typified as the professional sick person, who thinks of himself as such and contracts into the *habitus* of a sick person—the same processes holding true in the case of captivity or exile. Insofar as I hope, I release myself from an inner determinism comparable to a cramp, by which I risk—in a testing experi-

[4] Pages 29–67.

ence—settling into one of those degraded, fragmented, and finally somnambulistic expressions of the human person, which engenders despair above all because it involves fascination.[5]

This last remark seems to me of the greatest importance, because it underscores the obsessional character of despair.

At this point we may return to the idea that I expressed earlier when I pointed out the structural characteristics of the human being and of the human condition which allow for the insertion of freedom. As I said in some remarks I addressed, in 1937, to the International Congress of Philosophy, then convened in Paris: The fact that every one of us knows himself destined to die may expose us to the temptation to be hypnotized by this ineluctable deadline, and this thought of inevitable death which can overtake us at any moment can well degenerate into an obsession. But, more than that, if this obsession takes hold of us, if it possesses us in the strongest sense, it can make everything else seem devoid of meaning and colorless. When, some years ago, before the members of the Oxford Philosophic Society, I attempted to show that a sinister possibility is in a way implied by the fact that we are perishable beings, my listeners seemed scandalized, and I was told that such an attitude was morally reprehensible. But my critics were reasoning as moralists in a case where medical or clinical reflection would have been much more in order. If we find ourselves confronted by someone in the grip of this obsessive fear of death, can we for a moment suppose that there would be any sense in offering him moral remonstrances, or in telling him that his behavior is antisocial? It is only through love, of which one could offer him a living witness, that one would perhaps be able to free him from this obsession, or to give breath once again to this soul in the grip of spiritual asphyxia.

But on the philosophic level it is the business of reflection, as I attempted to show in 1937, to leave open the illusion

[5] *Homo Viator*, trans. E. Craufurd (London: Gollancz, 1951), p. 41.

embodied in the belief that the fact of our being destined for death implies for us an inner fatalism, when actually, if that obsession takes hold of us, it is with the complicity of our freedom—a freedom which abdicates before the ineluctable.

This is the moment for a study—never more necessary than in our own time—bearing upon the "essence of human freedom," to make use of a phrase employed by Schelling in his 1809 treatise,[6] which is perhaps his masterpiece and to which Heidegger freely refers today.

The philosophic context into which the reflection on freedom is brought into this chapter is likely to surprise the reader. He will ask why we need stress a connection between freedom and hope which does not seem apparent. Here, the controlling fact for me was that, as we have seen—particularly in a certain existential line of thought—an absolutely opposite relation was being articulated. When a philosopher like Sartre dares to write that man is condemned to be free, so that freedom is no longer treated as an achievement but rather as a radical deficiency, there is a great temptation to place freedom at the heart of despair, having only to invent some Marxist device in order to escape the dilemma thereby created. In an existential perspective of that kind one would be disposed to define the free man as the rootless man, knowing and wanting himself as such. This becomes apparent in the literature which we see around us by a peculiar sort of fraternization between the intellectual and the "beatnik," and it is only by exhaustive —though by no means deceptive—dialectical acrobatics that the anarchism so defined by this fraternity can be transmuted into a Marxism which, while certainly heterodox, will try in spite of everything to be accepted or tolerated by the orthodox Marxists.

It is not my intention to undertake a critique of this extravagant enterprise. I will merely observe that while a rigorous

[6] Philosophische Untersuchungen über das Wesen der menschlichen Freiheit," in *Philosophische Schriften*, vol. I (1809).

philosophic thought must find it intrinsically negligible, it is nevertheless of considerable interest from a psychosociological viewpoint, or, if you wish, for that existential psychoanalysis whose value Sartre, in *Being and Nothingness*, should be credited with bringing to light, without perhaps suspecting that it might be turned against the dogmatism to which he would subsequently, and surprisingly, subscribe.

Deliberately bracketing the enterprise in question, I would like to make explicit the nature of the relation which seems to me to exist between freedom and hope. This is all the more necessary since a very serious error can be made here, if, in mistaking the real characteristics of hope, we risk confusing with it the kind of vague and bewildered expectation that Gide, for example, celebrated in the *Nourritures terrestres*. In this perspective, freedom would be confused with the suggestibility of the dilettante who is in a certain way curious about everything, but without ever being ready to give himself, to devote himself, to anything. There is, to my mind, no more absurd caricature of what a free man is and must be.

To begin with, we must take note of the significant fact that not one of us can really say, "I am free." There is no meaning in the statement that man *is* free, and there is of course still less in claiming, with Rousseau, that he is *born* free; there is no more fatal error than that which consists in regarding freedom as an attribute. I am tempted to say that it is exactly the opposite. It is far more appropriate to say that every one of us has to make himself into a free man; that within the bounds of the possible he has to take advantage of the structural conditions of which I have spoken, which make freedom possible. In other words, freedom is a conquest—always partial, always precarious, always challenged. And we should remind ourselves again that it is in the midst of a situation of captivity that freedom can be born, at first in the shape of the aspiration to be free. But the word "aspiration" is misleading; it can correspond to a simple "I should like" which is separated

by an abyss from "I want" (*je veux*). And in fact we have
seen that hope is itself irreducible to aspiration, since it implies a patience, a vigilance, and a firmness of purpose which
are incompatible with a simple "I should like."

To say that the freest man is the one who has the most hope
is perhaps above all to indicate that he is the man who has been
able to give his existence the richest significance, or stake the
most on it. But this is enough to exclude absolutely the pure
dilettante, that is, the one who, living only for himself, seeks
solely to collect such experiences as will awaken in him, each
time with different shades and nuances, a feeling of exaltation
which fulfills him for that moment. But from such a flame,
can anything remain in the end but ashes?

In the line of thought that I have tried to formulate in the
course of this book, it is evident that the stakes I have alluded
to here can only be conceived of on the level of intersubjectivity, or, if you wish, fraternity, and perhaps everything that
has been said up to now will be clarified if we now postulate
that the freest man is also the most fraternal.

But this formula aquires its full meaning only if we bring
to light the implications of the word "fraternal." The fraternal
man is linked to his neighbor, but in such a way that this tie
not only does not fetter him, but frees him from himself. Now
what I have tried to show is that this freedom is of primary
importance, for each one of us tends to become a prisoner of
himself, not only in respect to his material interests, his pas-
sions, or simply his prejudices, but still more essentially in the
predisposition which inclines him to be centered on himself,
and to view everything only from his own perspective. The
fraternal man, on the contrary, is somehow enriched by everything which enriches his brother, in that communion which
exists between his brother and himself.

But it is not hard to see the role that hope plays here. For
to love one's brothers is above all to have hope in them, that is,
to go beyond that in their conduct which almost always be-

gins by bruising or disappointing us. And on the other hand experience undeniably shows that the hope which we put in them can help to transform them, while, inversely, if by our thought we enclose them in what strikes us as their nature, we contribute to stopping their spiritual growth. This is manifestly true for the educator. But there is a sense in which it may be said that fraternity implies a mutual education.

Moreover, it seems to me necessary to stress that fraternity excludes the spirit of abstraction and the ideologies in which that spirit tends always to be embodied. Here I come back to what I said before on the difference between equality and fraternity. It might be said that the spirit of abstraction always leads to a kind of segregation, the class segregation practiced in communist countries being in this respect no better than racial segregation. But what is fraternity if not the refusal of all forms of segregation? This refusal, of course, is actually the negative side of the emphasis placed on the universal. But the danger is ever-present, as I have shown, that the universal may wither or deteriorate into a purely abstract relation, and it is precisely to this deterioration that the spirit of fraternity is opposed. Again: fraternity implies a dynamism which is in fact that of love, and not—as with equality—that of the rectifying spirit. But this is of course no more than a schematic way of presenting an opposition which in concrete reality is not always clearly discernible.

Incidentally, in insisting as I have just done on the connection between fraternity and freedom, I do not claim to give an exhaustive account of the main characteristics by which the free man is defined. On the contrary, I think that one must have recourse to definitions of an apparently quite different order, and here I refer primarily to the attitude which a free man must have toward what is commonly called truth.

I was struck, a few years ago, by the concurrent testimony that I received in 1956 and 1957 about the conditions under which the well-known uprisings, first in Poland and then in

Hungary, took place. Witnesses affirm that in both countries it was the lies accumulated by the respective governments and by a servile press which were the last straw. In Hungary, in particular, I was told by a diplomat who lived for eight years in that country, that what the population rose against was the lie, and this, moreover, without being able to say precisely *in the name of what*, positively, the insurrection had taken place. Indeed it seems that the Hungarian insurgents knew much more clearly what they did not want at any price, what with their whole being they rejected, than what they would wish to put in the place of the hated régime.

In reflecting on the relation which might obtain in such situations as the foregoing between freedom—or, more precisely, liberation—on the one hand, and truth, on the other, I asked myself how one might define the positive counterpart of a protest against the lie that proved capable in a few days of transforming a capital, a whole country, into a battlefield.

Perhaps this counterpart is the will to be acknowledged— that same will which is wounded each time a person is humiliated. We may recall here the way in which Dostoievski in his major works could release the distinctive effects of humiliation. The lies which were cynically published in the Hungarian press, for example, were bound to be regarded as an insult by those who were supposed to accept them and to live by them, day after day.

But on reflection the will to be acknowledged must appear without question to be linked with truth, provided one is careful not to confound truth with what is only brute fact.

What is it that is *un*acknowledged here? It is not such data as might figure in a dossier at the back of some file; it is rather a certain quality which is implied in self-respect. Everything happens as if the oppressor proposed to strip the oppressed of his self-respect. And from what motive? To him it is simply a matter of transforming the individual into a tool which is incapable of opposing the ends pursued by the oppressor.

But self-respect comprises precisely that stubborn refusal to let oneself be degraded to the level of an instrument.

It is in this connection that the all-too-familiar techniques for obtaining a false confession from an accused person take on their sinister significance. These mendacious confessions, by which the prosecutor himself is not fooled, aim at the destruction from within of him who was yesterday an adversary but today a mere tool. The man who has been put under the compulsion of professing a lie, usually under the influence of torture or blackmail, is in fact dissociated from himself, stripped of that kind of consistency between what he is and what he says which is at the heart of his self-esteem as a man. That is what the expression "to break" means in this connection. The torturer, whatever the means he has employed, has made of his victim a slave, not only physically but morally. The man who has betrayed truth—and by that one must understand truth not as a meaningless abstraction, but as one's own truth—can no longer be a free man.

This observation sheds light on a great many situations beyond the one just evoked, however, for it is in this same manner that the representatives of a servile press are themselves somehow alienated. Henceforth they are literally without a home, so well expressed in the German word *heimatlos*.

One is bound to notice in this connection that the Marxists who, in the footsteps of their master, have so justly stressed the alienation of the proletariat, often appear incapable of discerning the moral forms of alienation. And when by chance they are able to recognize them, they become entangled in inextricable contradictions from which they manage to emerge only by a cynicism that often conceals a suppressed despair. This was the case, for example, with Bertold Brecht, as his recent biographer, Martin Esslin, has so well shown.[7]

[7] *Brecht: A Choice of Evils. A Critical Study of the Man, His Work, and His Opinions* (London: Eyre & Spottiswoode, 1959). Published in the United States under the title, *Brecht: The Man and His Work* (New York: Doubleday, 1960).

Reflection on what I have called "at-home-ness" allows us, further, to clarify some of the concrete conditions apart from which there is not and cannot be a freedom worthy of the name. The situation of the refugee may be brought to mind, even where it does not involve entire dependence on what is rather called public charity. What is characteristic in the plight of the refugee is that he is *en porte-à-faux* "without support." [8] This does not mean, simply, that he is not integrated into the community, but perhaps more exactly that just because he feels himself tolerated, after a fashion, he has to watch his words and even his very thoughts.

From a similar perspective, it must be said that the transfers of populations, which are multiplied in our day in countries which have the impudence to call themselves democratic, are crimes against humanity, for they too threaten that deep and distinctive need of man which consists in wanting not only his inner consistency but also an adjustment to his own milieu that shall be at least partly self-determined. This point seems to me to be particularly important because it puts us on guard against the idealist's temptation to identify truth with pure interiority. On this point Hegelianism and Marxism must be credited with having exposed an illusion which is today no longer tenable. But this in no way gives us license to go to the other extreme and neglect or minimize the role of subjectivity in favor of exclusive attention to the material conditions in which a man develops.

Nor should we take refuge in compromise formulas that are always deceptive. The truth is that it is impossible to conceive of freedom without emphasis on a whole congerie of conditions, so complex as to verge on the contradictory, which each of us is obliged both to experience and to dominate, without, however, cherishing the hope of being able to do so absolutely, whether with respect to oneself or to circumstances.

[8] *en porte-à-faux:* a French architectural expression the literal meaning of which is "overhang."

In this perspective, nothing seems more absurd than to treat freedom as an attribute, when it can never be more than a partial and precarious victory. To become aware of this, we have only to imagine the confusion into which each of us would be plunged if we were asked, "Are you free?" To such a question no answer is possible, because in fact the question is meaningless. It can only take on meaning if it becomes specific. Suppose, instead, that I am asked, "Do you consider that such and such a step was freely taken—for instance, with reference to your career?" Even in this case a reflection centered on the existential, that is, no longer obsessed with causality—an obsession from which contemporary thought, especially that of Bergson, has helped to free us—will bring to light the difficulties involved in trying to answer such a question honestly. Let us imagine, for example, the case of a man who, without any wish to do so, is obliged to study medicine merely because his father, himself aged or ill, has passionately desired his son to succeed him in the practice of that profession. If you should ask this young man, "Do you consider that you have freely chosen this profession?" he would no doubt be greatly embarrassed. He would certainly acknowledge having undergone pressure from his father, but it is possible that he would refuse absolutely to consider that pressure as a constraint, or *coactio*. Perhaps he would ascribe to affection or to a sense of duty what others would interpret rather as blackmail, and so he would refuse to admit that his choice was not a free one. But it must be understood as well—and this point seems to me most important, bearing as it does on what I have said previously in connection with *Un Homme de Dieu*—that perhaps in the actual content of life his own way of interpreting his choice in retrospect would be considerably modified. If his professional life is a failure, if he perceives that he should in fact have oriented his existence quite differently, it is probable that he will be inclined to lay stress, resentfully, on the pressure suffered, which would appear a posteriori as a constraint. The reverse would be the case if, having taken a liking to his work, he has on the contrary found success in it and is satisfied that his life has been worthwhile.

Along these lines, one might be tempted to say that the essential question can be formulated only in a personal form, and in the first person, and only from that moment where our life stretches behind us like a well-traveled landscape, reconstructing the progress—so often halting and problematic—that has been ours. At that moment, it seems to me, we can ask ourselves, "Am I conscious of having been a free man?" Certainly it is then that the question takes on meaning, although it is manifestly impossible to answer it by a simple yes or no.

IX ⤙

The Threat to Integrity

I T is perhaps appropriate that in this final chapter I should
ask myself the difficult and disturbing question which I
formulated at the end of the preceding chapter: Having come
to a point where almost all my life is behind me, can I in all
sincerity say that this life—my own—has been that of a free
man? Or, in other words, have I the impression that in the
course of this long existence the willed had pre-eminence over
the suffered? In the first place, I am aware that in principle it
would seem that I alone can decide the matter. How could
someone else—a commentator or a biographer—enter by
thought or imagination into my existence so as to answer the
question I have posed? On the other hand, reflecting on the
way in which I have formulated the question, I am obliged
to own that it is open to this criticism—that it seems to establish a relation of quantitative inequality between the willed
and the suffered; and one must ask whether, in this domain,
such a relation is really thinkable.

Pursuing my self-questioning, I wonder to what degree this
completed life, as I consider it to be, might appear to me today
as having *fulfilled*, or not, a certain initial choice. I realize that
it is impossible to answer this question in the affirmative, as
I would be able to do if ambition had been an overriding con-

sideration with me from the beginning—in other words, if I had been concerned to climb a certain number of stairs. In that event I could, like an Alpinist who has or has not climbed a certain peak which he wanted to be the first to scale, answer in an unambiguous way: Yes, I have (or, no, I have not) attained to such and such a height. Here, I am purposely ignoring the question of whether such a climb is not inevitably accompanied by a whole train of sorrows and disappointments which were scarcely imagined when setting out. And I might note in passing that the man whose acts are dictated by this kind of ambition is frequently the prisoner of an obsession and runs the grave risk of being unable at the end to regard himself as a free man. It seems, however, that when I had my whole life still ahead of me, it did not present itself to me as a ladder I had to climb—still less so since competition, as I had experienced it in my student days, has always appeared hateful to me. This fact, incidentally, explains in some degree perhaps the very special conditions under which my existence gradually unfolded. This does not mean, of course, that I was without ambition. To make such a disclaimer would be entirely deceitful. But this ambition could not be dissociated in any way from the profound need to proffer a certain word— and I quote here some verses from one of the *Grandes Odes* of Paul Claudel which to my view express in an incomparable way that kind of aspiration:

> Let me be among men as a person without face and my
> Word upon them without the least sound, like a
>   sower of silence, like a sower of shadows,
>   like a sower of churches,
> Like a sower of God's measure.
> Like a small grain of unknown kind
> Which, cast upon good earth, gathers from it all
>   its energies and makes a particular plant,
> Complete with roots and all.[1]

[1] From the ode entitled "La Maison Fermée," in *Cinq Grandes Odes*, 43rd ed. (Paris: Gallimard, Pleiad, 1948).

There is admittedly some pretention, some presumption, involved in daring to ascribe to oneself in some way the creative resolution which is expressed here by a poet of genius. But such terms as "sower of silence" and "sower of solitude" describe very well what I have tried to be, and, too, they make it possible to see just how difficult it is for me to answer the question I posed at the beginning. We are as far as it is possible to be from the case of the artist who can say, "My picture was recently sold for fifty million francs to the Galerie Charpentier," or, "My last play had a run of fifteen hundred performances," and so on. In other words, the response to such a vocation cannot, by definition, be computed in terms of measure, of number. What counts, and what moreover can be discerned only imperfectly by oneself, is the fact of one's having found an echo in very diverse people, often widely separated and scattered over the four corners of the earth. It is a question, however, whether these people constitute in any way that species of opaque and rather suspect entity which is called a "public." I would be less than honest if I did not acknowledge that this response has in a sense existed and exists, without there being any possibility of determining its amplitude or depth. There is in this area something which by definition escapes investigation or inquiry, in the same sense that an essential human relation does, be it one of friendship or of love.

Have I, then, achieved exactly what I wished? Surely it would be false to make that claim, if only because the end-result was unforeseeable in any case. But perhaps it would be proper here to make a distinction in depth between *wishing* and *willing*. Without any doubt I would have *wished* to be a dramatic author with a success comparable to Roussin or Anouilh; but what I *willed* was, no less clearly, incompatible with that sort of success, and I can at least say to myself that never, in any one of my plays or in any circumstance, have I deliberately sought to realize the conditions which would have made it possible for me to achieve this commercial success. And it is in no sense certain that even had I willed it I should have been capable of realizing my ambition.

So what I can recognize in retrospect as freedom's part seems to me to coincide with that of creativity itself. Actually, all sorts of questions can arise, not only about the nature of this creativity but also about its limits. Certainly it is not necessary to be a Marxist to recognize that the latter depended to some extent on the milieu in which I have lived, and I feel no embarrassment in admitting that this has been a bourgeois one, and that my dramatic characters have belonged to the milieu which was my own, not at all because they thereby enjoyed in my eyes any special prestige, but because this was the one which I knew from the inside. It would have seemed dishonest to me at any time to want to stage my plays in a setting which I knew only through hearsay or through reading. I must add that it will continue to be a source of regret to me, and to a certain degree even of remorse, not to have had contact with the working-class milieu, for example. This was not due to any wish of mine but was the result of circumstances, in particular the dubious state of health which exempted me from the obligation of military service. And here I would have to go into a host of details, both tedious and indiscreet in order to make clear, in the heart of an existence like my own, the inextricable entanglement of the willed and the suffered.

Turning now from this self-examination, I should like to consider briefly an objection which might justifiably be made in connection with the text of Claudel that I have quoted. Is there not a contradiction, one might ask, between what has been said earlier about fraternity and its pre-eminent value, and this concern to be a sower of solitude or of silence? The contradiction is, I believe, only apparent, or—more precisely —it implies a confusion to which I believe it is essential to call attention. The word "solitude" is ambiguous. It does not, in fact, mean isolation, for isolation is a lack, a deprivation,

whereas solitude is a fullness. In the world whose structure
is displayed about us, developing at a rate which is not that of
organic growth, we find human beings increasingly separated
from one another the more they are herded together. But this
promiscuous closeness that we see, for example, on beaches,
where people crowd in together during vacations, has nothing
to do with fraternity. And it is surely not by chance that it is
accompanied by an uproar so deafening that no one feels at
home. The same holds true for those enormous housing proj-
ects which spring up like mushrooms on the outskirts of big
cities; there, too, promiscuity and tumult prevail. My thought
would be best expressed by saying that solitude is as essential
to fraternity as silence is to music. We should remember that
fraternity is perhaps above all a form of respect, and that there
is no respect without distance, which in this case means that
every human being must have access to an interior space without which he withers like a plant, or a tree. Need we be reminded of this in the country of Thoreau and Emerson?

But we must also bear in mind that these truths are acknowledged less and less, or, more precisely, that forces are at work
which are tending to stamp upon existence a character such
that they can no longer be lived.

Here we touch upon the especially grave and agonizing
problem to which I would like to devote this final chapter,
well aware, however, that I shall not be able to supply anything in the nature of a solution. There are, I believe, profound reasons here which militate against the very notion of
"solution."

The problem in question is that of understanding what becomes of human dignity in the process of technicalization to
which man today is delivered over. Never, of course, have
such words as "human dignity," "the human person," and
so on, been more constantly enunciated, but to draw from
that a positive conclusion about any real situation to which
this language has reference would be to succumb to a strange

illusion. How can one escape the conviction that we are in fact witnessing a widespread deterioration which this sort of verbal inflation seems unconsciously aimed at compensating on a level of verbal pretence? What is certainly true is that we see today, heightened and generalized, a tendency to view any kind of service as incompatible with what I believe should be called a basic pretension. But the real problem is to know what relation this pretension bears to that concept which rightfully deserves the name of human dignity.

Of course there can be no denying that the exploitation of the servant by the master, as it has manifested itself through the centuries, rightly seems to us today to be unjustifiable. From that fact it does not at all follow that service itself should be considered humiliating. On this point many people have been the victims of a most unfortunate confusion. It would seem at present that each man intends to constitute—sometimes, but not necessarily always, with those whom he still calls his own people—a sort of island of autonomy which surely has nothing in common with the autonomy that Kant put at the heart of his ethic. Besides, the very term "autonomy" is inadequate here since it implies nothing in the nature of a self-imposed rule, but rather of a will to pleasure, the only restraint on tastes and inclinations being the fear of the law. This kind of self-enclosedness distorts to the point of contradiction Kant's rule of the autonomous practical categorical.

But it must be added at once—and this is probably the most noteworthy factor—that technology looms as more and more indispensable to the realization of the design of increasing uniformity, variations from which can only become progressively ineffectual. I cannot resist the temptation to quote here a few lines from an article by the Roumanian essayist E. M. Gioran, which have a diagnostic value: "So-called civilization teaches us how to take possession of things, when it should initiate us into the art of letting go, for there is neither freedom nor 'real life' without an apprenticeship in 'de-possession.'

I take hold of an object, I reckon myself the master of it; in fact, I am its slave, as I am equally the slave of the instrument which I manufacture and wield." Here I would introduce a distinction which Gioran seems inadvertently to overlook: To the degree that I manufacture the instrument, or simply contribute to its perfecting, it seems an exaggeration to say that I am its slave; in any case, I am much less so than he who only makes use of it.

From this digression we return to that idea which has been one of the basic themes of our whole inquiry, namely, that to some extent there is freedom wherever there is creation, even on the humblest levels. (This assertion, which appears to me necessary, does not significantly modify the diagnosis of Mr. Gioran.) The great majority of men are merely consumers and to that extent wholly dependent. They are thereby self-condemned to a new kind of slavery the true nature of which is, moreover, concealed from itself. Nor should we overlook the fact that this slavery is actually a consequence of the omnipresence of advertising, which is itself organically connected with industrial development. Those who produce television sets or refrigerators must be able to create an environment capable of absorbing them. All this has been said a thousand times and there is no need to stress it again. But it is none the less relevant in this context to ask what the by-products of such a situation may be, not only with reference to the behavior of human beings but to the way they consider and evaluate themselves. Now it is, in my view, a certainty—on which the German philosopher Gunther Anders, in his book, *Der Antiquiertheit des Menschen*,[2] has shed a brilliant light—that man is tending more and more to consider himself in relation to the products of his own techniques, and by a singular paradox he even undervalues himself in comparison with the far more precise and effective apparatus which his technical skill has perfected. This anomaly is an extension of

[2] Munich: Beck, 1956.

the prophetic insights which Samuel Butler articulated in his *Erehwon*. But this tendency is bound to have moral consequences that are incalculable, since that kind of self-appreciation—or, rather, self-depreciation—leads to the radical negation of the transcendence which classical philosophy, or one might even say *philosophia perennis*, attributed to the mind as distinct from the body. Actually, what tends to replace mind is the notion of a more or less rigorous technological function.

It goes without saying that up to now I have simplified the problem in a way which distorts contemporary human reality, in seeming to leave aside, or in only alluding to, the social side of this same reality. Even if one individual should have the illusion of really being the center, endowed with a self-sufficiency which technical progress aims to facilitate, it is all too plain that this illusion cannot for a moment withstand the pressure of fact. It is also clear that the simplistic notion of what we call "society" as merely the arithmetical sum of individuals is not a tenable one. Surely society has quite another character; it has generally the aspect of what Simone Weil called "the great beast," this expression having, if I am not mistaken, a Platonic origin. And this means that each of us, however he may desire to do *what he pleases*, is integrated into a certain totality, of which it must further be said that the diverse feelings which it inspires, ranging ordinarily between fear and aversion, scarcely seem any longer to carry with them that shade of admiration or of quasi-religious submission without which a philosophy of the state, however short of optimism, seems unable to take form.

Here the difficult question must be asked—namely, what relation should hold between the bureaucracy's development and the growing technicalization of which we are the witnesses, or even the victims? As always in matters of this kind, we should be wary of oversimplified conclusions. There is no doubt, for example, that bureaucracy can develop in the most extreme and paralyzing fashion in countries that are still technically underdeveloped. But on the other hand one may well fear—although such a development is not inevitable— that technocracy implies a tendency toward centralization, and that the operation of this central authority cannot be separated from a corresponding hypertrophy of offices and therefore of bureaucracy. I say that all this is perhaps not inevitable since we now have, for example, in France, a clear-sighted technocratic effort to achieve the industrial decentralization that is obviously needed. But it is also apparent that that effort is encountering the greatest difficulties, and, one may say, a sort of generalized ill-will on the part of the public, which tends increasingly to crowd into enormous urban centers under conditions that are least favorable for what a few years ago we would still have called the development of the individual. But this word "development" becomes really meaningful only if the integrity of the human being is considered as the central value—and it is precisely this integrity which is directly threatened today. Here we rediscover the problem formulated earlier, for I believe it is possible to show that integrity and dignity are terms which, though not identical, are indissolubly linked.

The notion of integrity is one which deserves a more complete elucidation than is generally given it. When we say that a man has integrity we usually want to emphasize the fact that he is absolutely honest, that there are in him no fissures through which temptation can enter. But the etymology of the word suggests that integrity has a more essential quality. As usual, the thought of the ancients is relevant here. The integrated man is master of himself; he is in perfect possession of himself. It must be added at once, however, that this does not in any sense imply complacency or self-sufficiency. I would even go so far as to think that the man who proudly proclaims this self-sufficiency usually suffers unawares from an inner wound or deficiency which he seeks in this way to compensate. But we cannot be sure that such was the case with some of the wise men of antiquity whose sociological and existential context was so far removed from our own. And I am willing to acknowledge that even today, here and there, might be found survivors of this mentality, the beneficiaries of exceptional conditions comparable in some measure to those more common in antiquity. But we cannot avoid being struck by the fact that in our world the men who claim self-sufficiency generally have recourse to modes of escape which are all too familiar, be they alcohol, drugs, or sheer speed, the latter patently taking on the character of alcohol, a drug, or quite simply, poison. But we can speak of integrity only where such escapism is systematically excluded. We are faced, then, with this question: In a world in the process of complete technicalization, does not such escapism appear less and less avoidable, which would imply that the integrity of which I am speaking is increasingly threatened?

Clearly, it is not a question here of implication in the precise sense of the term. Rather we should ask whether, in such a world, the individual is not increasingly in danger of succumbing to this temptation. Are we not in the presence of a universal alienation, taking this word in the widest sense, and not in the narrow meaning conferred on it by Marx and the Marxists? Alienation here refers to the fact that in a world increasingly under the hegemony of technology, the human being is undergoing what might be called an enucleation. Need I say that we are rediscovering here, transposed in the light of the most recent developments, the views which I formulated more than a quarter of a century ago, not in reference to technology but rather as a criticism of the hypertrophy of what is merely functional or functionalized. It might also be said, in a language that is convergent with the foregoing, that in such a world the life of each of us tends to lose its existential weight because circumstances which formerly would have been taken in their intrinsic seriousness now tend to be

interpreted in terms of adjustment or maladjustment. To take
only one example: if someone suffers too deep and too lasting
a grief after the death of someone near to him, there would
be no hesitation, in the contemporary framework I am speaking of, in calling the reaction a morbid one, and it is all too
clear that the morbid or the abnormal refers to a trespassing
upon certain rules of self-adjustment to the inevitable. We
should recognize that what is involved here is a sort of degradation of the stoicism of Epictetus or Seneca to the merely
functional level. Whatever one may think of stoicism—and
to me it has always seemed metaphysically rather shallow—
it none the less implies the affirmation of sovereignty, of a
hegemonikon, which occupies a place considerably above any
possible technique. There is no common ground between this
stoicism and an indistinguishable mixture ranging from a species of pelmanist gymnastics to some dubious residue of yoga.

What must be stringently insisted upon is that an anthropology with a functionalist commitment has no place for anything
in the nature of dignity, and if illusions can be entertained
on this point it is solely because language allows for anything,
because *anything can be expressed.* But we should be quick to
acknowledge that an anthropology of this order is not implied
by communist regimes alone, but tends to assert itself wherever a technocratic type of thought is affirmed, for such
thought tends inevitably to treat the human individual exclusively in terms of the return which he is likely to yield. And
what is this return if not a contribution to a certain world-
wide enterprise? But in what terms is that enterprise to be
conceived? Actually, as we know only too well, it runs the
risk of becoming itself the extravagant dream, or even the
criminal folly, of an individual or of a small group of men temporarily united by the same ambition. No doubt the objection
will be made that this is a phenomenon of social or historical
pathology, and that we ought nevertheless to rise to the conception of an entire society devoted to the pursuit of certain

ends. But it is precisely here that the problem re-emerges: For what is the nature and the value of these ends? *Who is a fit judge of their value?* And, on a deeper level, does the word "value" retain any meaning in such a context? It is only by fiction pure and simple that certain philosophers have given credence to the unfortunate notion that society, or a society, can be considered capable of positing values.

But all these assertions and questions, each of which opens the way to further ramifications, will, I think, be clarified by the following reflections. It is necessary to see what sort of self-image man fashions when he tends to picture the world in the light of the techniques that it has been given to him to invent. It is true that this image is more and more confused, misshapen, indecipherable, and that this distortion entails incalculable consequences for self-knowledge. The Socratic *gnôti seauton* was, after all, based on the idea of an identity of the knower and the known; and the principle of the identity of the ideal and the real thereby postulated was, in the last analysis, the foundation of the whole of traditional philosophy from Plato to Descartes to Hegel. But is not this postulate annulled, for all practical purposes, by the hyperbolic enlargement of technical skills—that is to say, of "know-how?" Does not the explosion of the objective world whose physiognomy is increasingly strange and threatening, entail in fact a pulverization of the subject? I mean to say that the techniques conceived on the model of those whose efficacy was demonstrated in the realm of nature will now be applied to the subject himself, who will, by the same token, cease to be treated as a subject. To realize this, we need only think of the experiments on the brain and of the psychic alterations they seem able to provoke. In such cases we are witnessing the constant and widespread violation of privacy which is without question one of the most alarming features of the present world. We need only recall, for instance, the scandalous "breaking and entering" which is involved in the use of what is, con-

tradictorily, called "truth serum"—as if truth in the pure and
noble sense of the word had anything to do with the possible
results of an injection of any kind. Surely it is not by chance
that such experiments were made with unprecedented enthu-
siasm and persistence by totalitarian regimes, of which it is not
enough to say simply that they are careless of truth, but rather
that truth for them is the prime enemy, for by its light the
inadmissible pretensions which operate in these regimes are revealed for what they are.

In this digression we have encountered once again that essential tie between man's dignity and the respect for truth
which I have tried to emphasize. Historically, those values
have always been in conflict with the same kind of sacrilege,
so that we may say without hesitation that the countless crimes
of which totalitarian dictatorships have been guilty should,
by a sort of salutary reversal, lead those who have retained
some lucidity of mind to become aware of these fundamental
interconnections, attention to which must inevitably have a
beneficial effect upon the whole human person.

Nevertheless, we must entertain no illusions here: this attention or reflection has increasing difficulty in operating today;
it is systematically discouraged—or, more precisely, whoever
makes an effort to guide his thought in this direction finds
himself exposed to a general strategy of intimidation which
is advanced now in the name of sociology, now, much more
absurdly, in the name of something which still claims to be
history but which is in fact a totally dubious by-product of
history. We are really witnessing a gigantic process of devaluation *of what is permanent in man* and above man, and the term
"desacralization," to which I have had frequent recourse in
my writings, seems the most accurate description of this process.

It would appear, then, that we should look exclusively in
the direction of a restoration of the sacred for what I must
stop short of calling a remedy for the situation I have tried

to describe. If I prefer not to speak of a remedy it is because by doing so one would risk slipping into a sort of pragmatism of the sacred, which would constitute an offense against the very thing one intended to restore. Here we encounter once again what I was alluding to at the beginning of this chapter when I said that we should beware of believing that such a problem is soluble. Perhaps what I mean will be clearer if we reflect on the meaning of a conversion worthy of the name, by which I understand an absolutely sincere and spontaneous conversion at the heart of an individual existence. Consider how absurd it would be to say to a convert: "You have found a solution to your difficulties," or, "You have found a remedy for your ills." It is not merely the words "solution" and "remedy" which are improper, it is the verb "to find" which is empty of meaning. The convert would undoubtedly reply: "I have not found, *I have been found.*" In other words, he would rightfully point out that everything is explained—or, more precisely, illuminated—by the idea of grace, and by the fact that he did not refuse that grace.

Here, however, the reader must be cautioned against any possible misinterpretation of my thought. If I have alluded to conversion it was simply to show how a certain kind of experience can take place beyond the level of solutions; I am by no means asserting that men will only be able to emerge from the impasse in which they are visibly caught on condition that they return to religion in its standard and confessional forms. To make such an assertion would be to fall into the pragmatism which I wish most to avoid.

Let us say, to begin with, that it would be not only presumptious but, properly speaking, absurd, to claim to be supplying anything in the nature of a formula. It is precisely the idea of a formula of any kind that I intended to challenge. The philosopher—and it is, after all, as a philosopher that I have been expressing myself in the course of this book, even, and perhaps most of all, when I have referred to my dramatic work—the philosopher must preserve himself completely from the temptation of the prophet's role; the man who wants to play the prophet is behaving as a charlatan, and here, as elsewhere, charlatanism in any form must repel us. I would concede, incidentally, that here the philosopher is obliged to exercise continuous vigilance, for he is constantly exposed to this pitfall. "But," some of my readers will ask, "when you venture to speak of grace, are you not in some sense open to the reproach which you have just invoked?" I have not the temerity or the complacency to demur categorically; as is so often the case, language here is suspect and perhaps incriminating. I readily acknowledge that the word "grace" is charged with all sorts of associations that carry the risk of unfortunate connotation. A whole literature of edification, whose intelligible content amounts to very little, tends to envelop in mist the author of such words. As always—yes, I venture to say always—it is experience and experience alone which has the last word here. The philosopher—and I would write the word without capitals—is the man who comes, not without trembling, to share with those who are willing to hear him out a certain experience which it was given to him to undergo. And of this experience he observes that no understanding can be achieved without taking account of that mysterious and essentially discrete reality which is called grace, and which is primarily defined, not merely by its irreducibility to freedom, but rather by the secret stimulus which emanates from it and without which it is likely that freedom itself would lose its meaning.

This would indicate—contrary to the opinion of those who, sometimes justifiably, have stigmatized the pride, the *hubris*, of the philosopher—that he has today the duty not merely to practice to the utmost the virtue of humility, which for obvious reasons is at the present time so generally discredited, but, further, that he must strive to bring into the open the redeeming value which it possesses, in a world where the manipulation of techniques in the service of the will to power threatens, in the absence of any counterweight, to engender pride, madness, and death.

This further implies that in my view the essential function of the philosopher is that of the sower, a function which probably cannot be performed except in the intimacy of the dialogue, *inter paucos*. And it is plain that in this connection it is to the lesson of Socrates that our thoughts necessarily turn.

I am writing these lines in the middle of the month of July 1961. In the course of these last weeks storm clouds have accumulated without respite on our horizons. None the less, something stubbornly assures us that the worst can yet be avoided without paying the price of a dishonorable capitulation the consequences of which could only be disastrous. This assurance is valid, for it is in the order not of desire, but of hope, as I have sought to define it. To attempt to silence it would be to shut ourselves within that circle of fatality which tends always to close around us but from which we must, day after day, release ourselves: we are men only on that condition.

To be men; to continue to remain men. These are the words on which I have concentrated unceasingly for twenty years. A Russian visitor told me recently that I was scathingly criticized recently in the leading Soviet literary journal, which accused me of being interested only in death, of being turned toward death, as is natural, I believe they said, for a representative of a bourgeois civilization in the final throes. I believe that the reader will have seen how absurd this accusation is. It is precisely my unconquerable love of life that precludes my subscribing to what I would call the "mortalism" of those for whom man finally breaks down like a machine.

These thoughts are perhaps particularly worth meditating upon in an hour when we have no assurance that millions or tens of millions of us are not destined for destruction. Even if the worst cannot be avoided—and it is not at all certain that it can be indefinitely—I believe that whatever may have been our shortcomings, our omissions—and I am by no means granting myself a blank check in the matter—we have to recollect with gratitude all that has been given us in our brief or long existence by a power which it seems to me unnecessary to name, as the token of a life worthy of the name—that is to say, a life both creative and fraternal. Creative and fraternal: it is with their union that I would like to close, as on a keynote in a Mozart quartet or symphony whose echo long re-echoes in us and remains not only in our ear, but in our heart; not only as a memory, but as a promise of eternity— the only eternity worthy of being hoped for and affirmed.

Author's Works Cited

Index

Author's Works Cited

Philosophical Works

Being and Having, trans. Katharine Farrer, Westminster: Dacre Press, 1949; Boston: Beacon Press, 1951. Published in French as *Être et avoir*, Paris: Aubier, 1935.

Le Déclin de la sagesse, Paris: Plon, 1954. Published in English as *The Decline of Wisdom*, trans. M. Harari, London: Harvill Press, 1954; Chicago: H. Regnery, 1955.

Du refus à l'invocation, Paris, Gallimard, 1940. To be published in the United States by the Noonday Press under the title *Creative Fidelity*.

Fragments philosophiques, 1909–1914, Louvain: Nauwelaerts, 1962.

L'Homme problématique, Paris: Aubier, 1955.

Homo Viator: Introduction to a Metaphysic of Hope, trans. E. Craufurd, London: Gollancz, 1951; Chicago: H. Regnery, 1951. Published in French as *Homo Viator: prolégomènes à une métaphysique de l'espérance*, Paris: Aubier, 1947.

"The Influence of Psychic Phenomena on My Philosophy," Society for Psychical Research (London), 1956. Twelfth Frederic W. H. Myers Memorial Lecture, 1955.

Man against Humanity, trans. G. S. Fraser, London: Harvill Press, 1952. Published in the United States as *Man against Mass Society*, Chicago: H. Regnery, 1952, and in France as *Les Hommes contre l'humain*, Paris: La Colombe, 1951.

Metaphysical Journal, trans. Bernard Wall, London: Barrie and Rockliff, 1952; Chicago: H. Regnery, 1952. Published in French as *Journal métaphysique*, Paris, Gallimard, 1927.

The Mystery of Being, trans. G. S. Fraser, London: Harvill Press, 1950–1951; Chicago: H. Regnery, 1950–1951. Published in French as *Le Mystère de l'être*, Paris: Aubier, 1951.

Philosophy of Existence, trans. M. Harari, London: Harvill Press, 1948; New York: Philosophical Library, 1949. Published in French as *Position et approches concrètes du mystère ontologique*. Introduction by Marcel de Corte. Louvain: Nauwelaerts, 1949.

Présence et immortalité, Paris: Flammarion, 1959.

Recherche de la famille; essai sur "l'être familial," G. Marcel *et al.*, Paris: Éditions familiales de France, 1949.

Royce's Metaphysics, trans. Virginia and Gordon Ringer, Chicago: Regnery, 1956.

Plays

Ariadne, trans. R. Heywood in B. Ulanov, *Makers of the Modern Theater,* New York, 1961, pp. 547–600. Published in French as *Le Chemin de crête,* Paris: Grasset, 1936.

La Chapelle ardente in *Trois Pièces* with *Le Regard neuf* and *Le Mort de demain,* Paris: Plon, 1931.

Le Cœur des autres, Paris: Grasset, 1921.

Les Cœurs avides (Le Soif), Paris: La Table Ronde, 1952.

Le Dard, Paris: Plon, 1938.

L'Emissaire, published in *Vers un autre royaume,* Paris: Plon, 1949.

La Grace, published with *Le Palais de sable* in *Le Seuil invisible,* Paris: Grasset, 1914.

L'Horizon, Paris: Spes, 1945.

Un Homme de Dieu, Paris: Grasset, 1925. Published in England in *A Man of God. Ariadne. The Funeral Pyre.* Three Plays with a Preface on the Drama of the Soul in Exile, London: Secker & Warburg, 1952. First American edition: *Three Plays: A Man of God, Ariadne, The Funeral Pyre,* New York: Hill and Wang, 1958.

L'Iconoclaste, Paris: Delamain, Boutelleau, 1923.

L'Insondable, published in *Présence et immortalité,* Paris: Flammarion, 1959.

Le Monde cassé, Paris: Desclée de Brouwer, 1933.

Le Quatuor en fa dièse, Paris: Plon, 1925.

Other Plays by Gabriel Marcel

Croissez et multipliez, Paris: Plon, 1955.

Le Fanal, Paris: Stock, 1936.

La Dimension Florestan, Paris: Plon, 1956.

Mon temps n'est pas le vôtre, Paris: Plon, 1955.

Rome n'est plus dans Rome, Paris: La Table Ronde, 1951.

Le Signe de la Croix, first published with *L'Emissaire* (see above) and separately (Paris: Plon) in 1961.

Le Théâtre Comique, which includes four plays: *Colombyre,* or *Le Brasier de la Paix; La Double Expertise; Les Points sur les I; Le Divertissement posthume.* Paris: Albin Michel, 1947.

Index

Abel, Niels Henrik, 13
Absolute Knowledge (concept of), 22
Absolute Self (concept of), 101
Abstraction, 13–14, 20–22, 23; "spirit of," 123, 124, 148; and ethics, 47–48
Admiration, necessity of, 126
Alain (Emile-Auguste Chartier), 27, 140
Alienation: concept of, 96; in modern society, 150–151, 163
Anders, Gunther. *See* Stern, Gunther
Anouilh, Jean, 156
Anxiety, 16–17, 103
Appearance and Reality. See Bradley, Francis H.

Bach, Johann Sebastian, 26
Beethoven, Ludwig von, 26, 120
Being: definition of, 76–78, 83, 88–89; and sensation, 44–45; and fidelity, 64, 65–66; vs. having, 97–98. *See also* Existence
Being and Having, 64, 69, 74, 80, 82
Being and Nothingness. See Sartre, Jean-Paul
Belief, 72–73, 99–100, 113; and solidarity, 133–134. *See also* Faith
Bergson, Henri, 1, 2, 19, 35, 42, 76, 128, 152
Berkeley, George (Bishop), 111
Betrayal, 64–73 *passim*, 120
Body: and the "I," 45–47; possession of, 97, 98
Blondel, Maurice, 23
Blum, Léon, 114
Bradley, Francis H., 21, 22, 41
Brecht, Bertold, 150
Brunschvig, Leon, 25, 27, 42
Buber, Martin, 4, 39
Bultmann, Rudolph, 72

Bureaucracy, 161ff. *See also* Mass society
Butler, Samuel, 161

Cain, Seymour, 82
Chapelle ardente, La, 62, 103–107
Chemin de crête, Le, 61, 107, 111–113, 115
Claudel, Paul, 155, 157
Cœur des autres, Le, 62
Cœurs avides, Les, 134, 137
Communism, 123
Commitment: political and ideological, 36, 119–122; unconditional, 71–72, 74
Compassion, 106–107, 134–135, 137
Concreteness (experience), 14–15, 20–21, 96
Conversion, 167
Corneille, Pierre, 143
Creativity, 126–127; in philosophy, 9–13 *passim*
Curel, François de, 28

Dard, Le, 116–122, 125, 126
Death: significance of, 136–139, 144–145; fear of, 144
Dehumanization, in modern society, 123–124, 139, 149–150, 163–169 *passim*
Delbos, Victor, 19
Desacralization, in modern society, 73–74, 166
Descartes, René, 14, 16, 86, 165
Despair vs. hope, 142–144, 150
Dialogue, 38–41, 169. See also *Interrogation*
Dostoievsky, Feodor, 149
Dramatic creation: its relation to philosophical formulation, 5, 28, 50, 60–62, 103, 107–108, 113, 115, 117